The
HOLINESS
GOD OF

livinglightministries.net

THE WHIRLWIND

The
HOLINESS
GOD
OF

BILL CRAMPTON

TATE PUBLISHING
AND ENTERPRISES, LLC

The Holiness of God
Copyright © 2016 by Bill Crampton. All rights reserved.

No part of this publication may be reproduced, stored in a retrieval system or transmitted in any way by any means, electronic, mechanical, photocopy, recording or otherwise without the prior permission of the author except as provided by USA copyright law.

Scripture taken from the *New King James Version*. Copyright © 1982 by Thomas Nelson, Inc. Used by permission. All rights reserved.

This book is designed to provide accurate and authoritative information with regard to the subject matter covered. This information is given with the understanding that neither the author nor Tate Publishing, LLC is engaged in rendering legal, professional advice. Since the details of your situation are fact dependent, you should additionally seek the services of a competent professional.

The opinions expressed by the author are not necessarily those of Tate Publishing, LLC.

Published by Tate Publishing & Enterprises, LLC
127 E. Trade Center Terrace | Mustang, Oklahoma 73064 USA
1.888.361.9473 | www.tatepublishing.com

Tate Publishing is committed to excellence in the publishing industry. The company reflects the philosophy established by the founders, based on Psalm 68:11,
"The Lord gave the word and great was the company of those who published it."

Book design copyright © 2016 by Tate Publishing, LLC. All rights reserved.
Cover design by Niño Carlo Suico
Interior design by Gram Telen

Published in the United States of America

ISBN: 978-1-68270-789-0
1. Religion / Christian Life / Spiritual Growth
2. Religion / Christian Life / General
16.02.22

Contents

1. The Cross 7
2. Roots 17
3. The Whirlwind 27
4. Believe 37
5. Old Man (Nature), Die! 51
6. New Man, Live! 61
7. Indians to the Rescue 69
8. The Favor of Esther 81
9. It's A New Day 89
10. Cannonballs 101
11. 11/11 113

1

The Cross

My God, My God, why have You forsaken Me? Why are You so far from helping Me, and from the words of My groaning? O My God, I cry in the daytime, but You do not hear; and in the night season, and am not silent. But You are holy, enthroned in the praises of Israel. Our fathers trusted in You; they trusted, and You delivered them. They cried to You, and were delivered; they trusted in You, and were not ashamed. But I am a worm, and no man; a reproach of men, and despised by the people. All those who see Me ridicule Me; they shoot out the lip, they shake the head, saying, "He trusted in the Lord, let Him rescue Him; let Him deliver Him, since He delights in Him!" But You are He who took Me out of the womb; You made Me trust while on My mother's breasts. I was cast upon You from birth. From My mother's womb You have been My God. Be not far from Me, for trouble is near; for there is none to help. Many bulls have surrounded Me; strong bulls of Bashan have encircled Me. They gape at Me with their mouths, like a raging and roaring lion. I am poured out like water, and all

My bones are out of joint; My heart is like wax; it has melted within Me. My strength is dried up like a potsherd, and My tongue clings to My jaws; You have brought Me to the dust of death. For dogs have surrounded Me; the congregation of the wicked has enclosed Me. They pierced My hands and My feet; I can count all My bones. They look and stare at Me. They divide my garments among them, and for My clothing they cast lots. But You, O Lord, do not be far from Me; O My strength, hasten to help Me! Deliver Me from the sword, My precious life from the power of the dog. Save Me from the lion's mouth and from the horns of the wild oxen! You have answered Me. I will declare Your name to My brethren; in the midst of the assembly I will praise You. You who fear the Lord, praise Him! All you descendants of Jacob, glorify Him, and fear Him, all you offspring of Israel! For He has not despised nor abhorred the affliction of the afflicted; nor has He hidden His face from Him; but when He cried to Him, He heard. My praise shall be of You in the great assembly; I will pay My vows before those who fear Him. The poor shall eat and be satisfied; those who seek Him will praise the Lord. Let your heart live forever! All the ends of the world shall remember and turn to the Lord, and all the families of the nations shall worship before You. For the kingdom is the Lord's, and He rules over the nations. All the prosperous of the earth shall eat and worship; all those who go down to the dust shall bow before Him, even he who cannot keep himself alive. A posterity shall serve Him. It will be recounted of the Lord to the next generation, they will come and declare His righteousness to a people who will be born, that He has done this. (Psalm 22, NKJV)

And the Lord God commanded the man, saying, "Of every tree of the garden you may freely eat; but of the tree of knowledge of good and evil you shall not eat, for in the day that you eat of it you shall surely die."… Then the serpent said to the woman, "You will not surely die. For God knows that in the day you eat of it your eyes will be opened, and you will be like God, knowing good and evil." So when the woman saw that the tree was good for food, that it was pleasant to the eyes, and a tree desirable to make one wise, she took of its fruit and ate. She also gave to her husband with her, and he ate. Then the eyes of both of them were opened, and they knew that they were naked; and they sewed fig leaves together and made themselves coverings. And they heard the sound of the Lord God walking in the garden in the cool of the day, and Adam and his wife hid themselves from the presence of the Lord God among the trees of the garden. Then the Lord God called to Adam and said to him, "Where are you?" So he said, "I heard Your voice in the garden, and I was afraid because I was naked; and I hid myself." And He said, "Who told you that you were naked? Have you eaten from the tree of which

> I commanded you that you should not eat?"...Also for Adam and his wife the Lord God made tunics of skin, and clothed them. (Genesis 2:16–17, 3:4–11a, 21; NKJV)

God's prophetic act, killing an animal, shedding blood to provide a covering for man—which ultimately became God giving His Son Jesus on a cross as a sacrifice for us—provides a covering and takes away the shame of our nakedness so that we can be restored to full fellowship with Him.

I also wonder if this is where man learned to eat meat, kind of like God's first barbecue. The code of ethics for every good hunter is you only kill what you plan to eat, so I don't think God was letting anything go to waste.

What is God's definition of *shame*? My answer to that is anything that we embrace that causes us to die. Adam's shame came when he ate from the tree that God told him would bring death. I often wonder why we are ashamed of being naked. I believe it is because we are so connected mentally, physically, and spiritually that if there is anything wrong in us, we instinctively know that we are less than what we really should be.

This book is not going to be about shame; I have seen something about Jesus that I wanted to share. Just recently I was at a worship meeting, and God showed me, in a vision, something so beautiful about shame that I had not seen before. In the spirit, He had been taking me back to the day of His crucifixion. It's like I was there living in that moment, and I hope I can present it the way I saw it. But first, I have to build a foundation of what was going on there.

In Jesus's life, did He ever experience shame? I know that He was looked down on because He was conceived out of wedlock, but was He ashamed by it? He knew who His Father was from His mother's womb. He was absolutely without sin, and a lamb without blemish. Would He have been embarrassed if He was ever caught naked? He was the second Adam, but He wore clothes.

When Jesus became a man, He wasn't God in just a body; He was God in His body, forever connected just like we are in our bodies. When His body hurt, He hurt. When His body was cold, He was cold. When someone touched Him with a warm hand, He felt their love. So when He got beat up and hung on a cross, He was beat up and hung on a cross.

Let's go back and look at what was happening at the cross. His people rejected Him. His disciples abandoned Him. He's been punched, beaten up, His beard pulled out, and a crown of thorns drove into His head. The skin on His whole body was ripped apart from flogging, exposing His bones. Men spit on Him as they passed by and mocked Him. His hands and feet have spikes driven through them. His arms and shoulders were popped out of joint.

He has to stand on the nails in His feet until He can't bear the pain anymore; then He has to let Himself hang from the nails in His hands to take the weight off His feet. But He can't hang on His hands very long because that pulls the muscles up under His lungs, suffocating Him, so that He has to stand on the nails in His feet again.

All of our sin has been put on Him, and the Holy Spirit has left Him, leaving Him feeling totally abandoned by God, which He has never known. He was stripped of clothes, and with our sin came our shame. Now He does know the shame of nakedness for everyone to see. I think Jesus knew shame beyond what anybody could imagine, and yet He despised it for us.

Satan is there with all his demons, and you can imagine the torment he's putting Him through, and there is no mercy. Jesus is now the devil's trophy stuck up on a hill by Jerusalem for the whole world to see. The Son of God reduced to being worth no more than a worm by those He created and loved.

But, in my vision, out of everybody who's there is Mary Magdalene, Jesus's saving grace. She is a true hero, a true representative of the church of God, a true bride of Christ—who once stood before Jesus in all of her shame, and He loved her and delivered her. Now He hangs before her, beaten to a pulp, totally humiliated and exposed. But she loves Him and rises above all of His shame and humiliation and is there for Him. The two of them face-to-face, in a moment of eye-to-eye contact, seeing past each other's shame, and deeply loving each other with a holy love. Then she gives Him His grace and returns to the other women who were back at a distance.

That's an example of the way it is to be with us. That is a secret of Christianity: running to God instead of from God. Jesus knows what it is like to experience shame. He went through it for us, to meet with us, and take us above it so that we can live in a new resurrected life. Even when we are in sin that's dominating us, and we can't get free, we need to run to God. He will get us out of it even if sometimes it's step-by-step in the midst of it. He makes our crooked places straight. Nothing separates us from the love of God. When we run to Him, we find Him. It's more of a shame to run from Him, and besides, He will hunt us down and find us anyway.

When do we see Jesus in His suffering? It's when we help the person who is in theirs, which really is when we help each other. It's hard to comprehend that Jesus becomes us when we are in our own humiliating tough times and need help. In fact, when we connect with a person in their suffering, by relating through our past suffering, it turns our suffering into a good thing. Maybe that's why Jesus appeared to Mary first after His resurrection because they were strengthened at the cross, transcending it, and making the cross a good thing. So Jesus died to cover our shame, and we live to cover His.

When the Son of Man comes in His glory, and all the holy angels with Him, then He will sit on the throne of His glory. All the nations will be gathered before Him, and He will separate them one from another, as a shepherd divides his sheep from the goats. And He will set the sheep on His right hand, but the goats on the left. Then the King will say to those on His right hand, "Come, you blessed of My Father, inherit the kingdom prepared for you from the foundation of the world: for I was hungry and you gave Me food; I was thirsty and you gave Me drink: I was a stranger and you took Me in; I was naked and you clothed Me; I was sick and you visited Me; I was in prison and you came to Me." Then the righteous will answer Him, saying, "Lord, when did we see You hungry and feed You, or thirsty and give You drink? When did we see You a stranger and take You in, or naked and clothe You? Or when did we see You sick, or in prison, and come to You?" And the King will answer and say to them, "Assuredly, I say to you, inasmuch as you did it to one of the least of these My brethren, you did it to Me." Then He will also say to those on His left hand, "Depart from Me, you cursed, into the everlasting fire prepared for the devil and his angels: for I was hungry and you gave Me no food; I was thirsty and you gave Me no drink; I was a stranger and you did not take Me in, naked and you did not clothe Me, sick and in prison and you did not visit Me." Then they also will answer Him saying, "Lord, when did we see You hungry or thirsty or a stranger or naked or sick or in prison, and did not minister to You?" Then He will answer them, saying, "Assuredly, I say to you, inasmuch as you did not do it to one of the least of these, you did not do it unto Me." And these will go away into everlasting punishment, but the righteous into eternal life. (Matthew 25:31–46, NKJV)

Here's another thing that I've seen about Jesus becoming a man. In the first chapter of Genesis, God established a law that says, "like produces after like." Then He created man after His own image. Later, when the Holy Spirit overshadowed Mary to conceive Jesus, how alike must man be for God to reproduce through her and not violate His own law? And now that Jesus is raised from the dead and we are born again, how alike to Jesus must we be with our new spirit being created in His image. That is very important to know because it helps us to learn the difference between our old man nature and new.

2

Roots

Writing that first book seemed to have taken everything out of me. Letting people know how I think gets overwhelming at times, but I have been accepted, and I've gotten somewhat more courageous. I really don't know how to write. I'm a two-finger typist and doing my best to remember. My lowest moment in writing so far has been getting edited. Street people can read my stuff and get everything I've said, but educated people seem to get confused, and I have to figure it out.

God has done a lot with me over the last few months, a lot of healing. I had gotten a motel to rebuild in my old hometown, and it was really good being there. The last time I worked there, I felt so much shame from what I used to be like that I never wanted to go back again. But this time, God restored a lot of things, and when it came time for me to leave, I did not want to go.

I got to speak at the prison here a couple of times too, and I loved it. But it was harder than I thought it would be. They were great, but my fear of speaking gets overwhelming. They took a lot of my books, and I got invited to go back.

I just had to get the courage to do it. Then the couple who invited me moved away, so it came to an end.

I don't know if I have the gift of interpreting dreams. I thought I was going to go a different route in this book than dreams, but God talks to me in dreams. I did pray about it, and it seemed the answer I got was Jesus continuously spoke to the people in parables. For me, I think, when God gets ready to do something in my life, to teach me something, He gives me a dream that will parallel what He's going to do. That way He has my attention. Then when it happens, it all makes sense, and I realize that He is in control.

Well, I had this dream, and I was told to write it, so I did, and writing it wasn't so bad. I think it is going to be the theme of what God is telling me to write in this book. I think this is going to be an adventure in God's further revelation of His Holiness. I still have no idea what this book is going to be about. I'm just writing. I do know that this is not a game. There are a lot of good books out there by people who know way more than me, so I'm not out to waste anybody's time. I really want to hear and give a clear word from God that will bring life to you and me. Jesus said in the book of John that it's the Spirit's words that bring life.

I had a dream that I was traveling through a place like a forest that had a lot of streams and rivers running through it. I was traveling alone, but I was running into people from time to time. I was really guarded about running into them

The Holiness of God

and letting them travel with me. None of them were people I knew, and I didn't know what they really wanted from me.

There was a gal who wanted to join up with me, but I did not trust her. I chose to leave without her, and as I was passing by where she was camped, I overheard her talking to her dad about me. I listened to hear what she was saying. She was talking good about me, and I knew she didn't want to use me, but I went on my journey anyway without her. Then I came to a waterfall at a river that I had to cross, and I went across it, leaving behind the forest.

The next place I was in was a big building. I was walking through the halls, and it seemed like a college university. The classes were getting out, and the students were filling the halls. As I walked by this one class, the teacher was standing at the door while his students were leaving. I knew the teacher, and I knew he was a good teacher.

He was a Native American Indian in the true sense of the word. The words *ancient of days* is what I sensed about him. It was like he was alive and lived here before the white man came to America. He could teach the true history of what happened in America and about God's involvement. I really longed to take his class, but I wasn't there to go to college, so I moved on.

My destination in this building was to find God, and I knew where He was. I made it to the room I was searching for, and I was right in the heart of God. The room had a recliner chair in the middle of it. It had a really relaxed atmosphere; I kicked back in the chair, with my legs up, and then waited for God to show up.

The room was really small; it seemed like I could reach out and touch all four walls from my chair, and there was a large window in front of me that had no glass in it. It was all open, like I was on the top of the building.

I was waiting for God, and nothing was happening. The walls weren't glowing, and there was no "presence," kind of like when you know you're in God's will but you don't sense Him at all. I knew I was in the heart of God because there was no other place I could go to get any closer to Him.

Then, all of a sudden, I went into a vision through that open window. God took me to a small patch of land that had a sagebrush plant growing out of it. He told me to pull up the sagebrush and look at the root. I grabbed hold of it and pulled it up, revealing one side of the root. That whole side was just one thick white clean root that went deep into the ground. God said that this was good. Then He told me to turn it over and look at the other side of the root, so I did.

That side of the root was dark and dirty. It was made up of hundreds of individual roots, like thin curly hair, and had bugs and spiders living in-between them. The roots were real shallow, and the bugs living in-between them gave it a sense of being like a spider's nest. Then God said that this was not so good.

The next thing I knew, I was translated into the living room of that Indian teacher I had seen earlier. I knew I was there for him to teach me what this vision meant, and I knew I was going to be there for a while. I had a big problem though; I could not breathe there. It was like there was no air, and I was holding my breath. I was really good at holding my breath for a long time, but I was getting down to about my last mouthful of air. Then he asked how I was doing; he knew I couldn't breathe there. I motioned to him that I was about as far as I could go.

He did not live on money, but he gathered some change together and gave me two dollars in quarters. He told me that this would buy enough air for me to last until a lady he knew got home. She was at work, and when she got home, he would get some money from her and buy me enough air for however long I needed. I was getting the shakes and felt the relief when he put the quarters in my hand, like an alcoholic getting a couple of beers to make it through the next few hours. I started breathing regular again, and then I woke up from the dream.

I looked up *sagebrush* on Wikipedia. One part says,

> Native Americans used sagebrush administered internally as a medicine to halt internal bleeding caused by battle wounds and child birth. The plant is very toxic to internal parasites and was used to expel worms. The plants oils are toxic to the liver and digestive system of humans if taken internally,

> with the toxic symptoms subsiding 24–48 hours after ingesting the plant. A tea made from sagebrush was used internally and as a topical dressing to treat infections by Native Americans in the Mountain West of North America. Woven sagebrush was used to make sandals in prehistory.

It said earlier that it's not good for most animals to feed on sagebrush, but sheep can feed on it in *moderation*.

I can really spiritualize on this. How many of us have had battle wounds from warfare in and out of the church? How many have worked hard and made a lot of sacrifice to bring someone into the kingdom, and it all went bad? What about the things in our lives that rob us of our nourishment, and infections that keep making us sicker and sicker?

I think some of the things I'm going to say will offend some people, but it won't kill you. A lot of what I'm going to say really isn't for food, but in *moderation*; it's more of a medicine. And hopefully, I can provide something for you to walk on.

I am a carpenter by trade. I love building new construction, but most of my work is in remodeling. I have to tear out the old and replace it with the new. Sometimes tearing out the old is really gross and sickening, but it has to be done, no matter how uncomfortable it is. But once the job is finished, then it all becomes worth it. With God's help, I can be a good carpenter, but I am still constantly

The Holiness of God

learning. I've been doing this for about thirty years now, about as long as I've been a Christian.

The same is how it is with us. God tears out all of the old and rebuilds us with the new. He is an excellent craftsman, He knows everything, and He makes no mistakes. For us, the cross really is a good place, putting down our old nature, and raising the new. It's constantly an ongoing process, and at times it is hard; but becoming like God, and getting closer to Him, is worth it.

The biggest focus of this dream was on the roots. I believe the roots are the church, corporate and individual. Probably the thing that I am going to be saying over and over in these books is that the church needs to come into unity. I am telling you, this is a serious issue with God. I hear so many excuses, and it's almost like calling evil good. I do know that unity is there in us. You can especially see it in Christian music events. Everybody comes together to worship Jesus, and nobody is divided into different denominational sections. It's when we get into our doctrines that we divide from each other. It's kind of like when we eat from the tree of life, we come together; but when we eat from the tree of knowledge, we separate.

In every church I've been in too, there's been a core group of people who are dedicated. They show up at prayer, Bible studies, etc., and are deep into the things of God, and they want unity. But there are others who listen to too many voices that tell them to be separate. This is what creates the space between us that allows the bugs and spiders to live in. As long as we keep listening to them, thinking that we are hearing from God, calling good evil and evil good, we will never be strong and healthy.

Something has to come and exterminate the bugs, bind us together, bandage us up, pour in the oil and the wine until we heal, and all become one root, deep and strong. It is going to happen.

God is going to do something big, and my purpose is to give you a heads-up. Take what I say, put it on a shelf, and when it happens, remember. I know it seems too big, but I've been reading about past revivals, and because of what happened in them happened to me, I know it can happen on an even greater scale.

I want to tell you something that is important: God is not interested in an earth that has become nothing but a baby factory for populating hell. He does not take pleasure in anybody's death that goes to hell. He loses, He loses the person whom He did have a future for. It's not going to stay like this. He does have a plan.

Even though Jesus is coming as the Lion from the tribe of Judah, He is still the Lamb sitting on the throne. There is a fierceness, but at the same time a gentleness. Like King David mourning over the death of his son Absalom, even though Absalom wanted his throne and him dead. I see Jesus reaching out with grace that is beyond grace.

Something is going to happen that is going to shake this entire world and force the church to come together.

This is a page out of a book that was given to me as a prophetic word about sixteen years ago. I don't know what book it came out of, but I taped the page into the front of my Bible, and I have believed it since. This is what it says,

> The Last Great Outpouring
>
> Behold, ye stand on the threshold of a new day. For I have truly great things in store for thee. Yea, thou hast not power to conceive that which I am about to do. For I shall bring to pass a new thing. Thou shalt rejoice exceedingly. Ye have heard of the showers, but I say unto thee that I shall send a mighty downpour. Many have cried unto Me out of hungry hearts and have received of My fullness and seen My glory: but I say unto thee, that in the day of the great deluge that is about to come, many shall come to know the reality of my power who have up until now not even dreamed of such a thing.
>
> Many who are scoffers, and many who are honest doubters shall find themselves swept away on the swelling tide of the outpouring of the Holy Spirit. For this is the time of the last great outpouring. This is the day of the preparation for the coming of the Lord. Many shall rejoice together in the Spirit's work who now are even at sword's point over doctrinal disputations and barriers of tradition.

But let thine heart be encouraged; for a new day is dawning: a day of repentance and a day of gathering for My people, saith the Lord. For they shall not continue barricaded and isolated behind walls of prejudice. I am the LORD, and I will be worshipped in spirit and in truth, and not in the bigotry of sectarianism and narrowness of denominationalism. The world is waiting for a robust Church to minister to its needs; and how can an ailing, dismembered Body bring healing to a sick and dying world?

Surely I will pour out My Spirit, and by prophecies, by signs and wonders, by many different types of miracles, and by healings, I will reaffirm the veracity of My Word and bring the message of the Gospel of Redemption to many who would otherwise never give heed. I am the Alpha and the Omega. Stand firm in Me. Never waver.

Be faithful regardless of apparent failures and discouragements; for my word shall surely be fulfilled, and thine eyes shall see Revival in proportion like as has never been witnessed before in the history of the human race.

Keep your eye on the end of the course. Victory is secured already. Do not let the hurdles cause thee consternation. Stay in the running. Verily, I am at thy side. According to each day shall thy strength be; and the race is not to the swift, but the obedient shall receive the prize.

3

The Whirlwind

> God is jealous, and the Lord avenges: the Lord avenges and is furious. The Lord will take vengeance on His adversaries, and He reserves wrath for His enemies: the Lord is slow to anger and great in power, and will not at all acquit the wicked. The Lord has His way in the whirlwind and in the storm, and the clouds are the dust of His feet. (Nahum 1:2–3, NKJV)

I did have a dream once about a tornado that I believe was a dream from God. I dreamed that I and a Christian friend of mine were in a house that was out in the country. The house was full of teenagers, like they were having a party. At first, I was uncomfortable being around them because I didn't know if they were a rough rebellious bunch or not.

I wanted to go through the house to the front porch, and we went to make our way through them. They stepped aside, being respectful, and let us pass. As I passed, I could hear them behind me cough with that smoker's hack you get when you've smoked too much pot, so I knew they were still rebellious teenagers.

We made it to the front porch and sat down. It was a clear beautiful blue summer day. I was just sitting there admiring the country when a gentle breeze picked up. But this breeze was different; it made the fence lines and power lines have a whistle to them, and the breeze wasn't blowing hard enough to cause that, but it was still happening.

I thought this was strange and wondered what it could be. I got up from my chair, walked to the side of the porch, and looked to the back of the house. To my horror, I saw a giant tornado coming. There was a mountain behind the tornado, and the tornado was as wide as that mountain, and it was here.

I ran to the front door to tell those kids about the tornado, and that we needed to get into the basement *now*, but they just looked at me. There was no time to show them the tornado, and they were too rebellious to listen to me. I went into horror of what to do, and then I woke up.

That's where it seems I'm at right now. I hear the whistling, and I sense something really big is coming. On one hand, to the rebellious, it is going to be really devastating; but to those who have eyes to see and ears to hear, it is going to be really good.

I've gotten two meanings out of this dream: one came pretty quick, but the second came over some time. I will start with the second one first because it flows with the last chapter. It's about the church.

I was walking home one time, and I was walking past a church that I didn't recognize. As I looked over to see what denomination it was, I felt God said, "Not one stone will be left standing." Then a series of things happened through the rest of that day that reminded me of this dream, and then I felt like God was giving me the interpretation to what He was saying.

The teenagers represent the church. Smoking pot represents winds of doctrine. The Church has become like what God called Israel, "a rebellious house" that's gotten so high on their winds of doctrines, tickling ears, that sound doctrine is getting lost. The tornado represents a tremendous storm that is coming, and the mountain represents a massive amount of strength behind it. Getting back to our foundation is going to be where our safety is, but how many people will listen before it's too late. It's going to be devastating if "not one stone is going to be left standing."

The first meaning I got was about this younger generation. It doesn't take a rocket scientist to figure out that the world is falling apart. Each generation is getting worse than the last. It really bothers me now of the kind of world we are leaving for our young people. If they don't grab hold and turn their generation around, what is going to happen?

The prison that I was invited to speak at was a women's prison, and one time after leaving there, God told me that most of the women in prison don't belong there. That women are there was because men have failed to be men; therefore, women are failing to be women. Parents are failing their children, and their children grow up and continue the cycle. It goes clear back to Adam and Eve. He said that "women have to forgive men and release God's kingdom to them." And that became my topic when I spoke there the last time, and they understood it and received it. A lot of forgiving and healing happened that meeting, and I know that is one of the keys.

When I was in jail, it seemed like jail was really just a big day care center for a bunch of rebellious little boys who needed a good spanking, including me. Ask any guy who's been in jail. Breaking my rebellion is what finally turned me around. I'm ashamed now at who I was, but I could not see it then.

God told me once, "Time and eternity have kissed." Since then, I've always pondered on what that meant. He gave me a start of an interpretation when He told me this. He told me that a dividing line is coming to the earth. Eternity is invading time. People are going to be judged when this line crosses over them with an eternal judgment.

If they reject the Gospel when this line crosses over them, they will be permanently sealed, like the fallen angels, no longer allowed to be granted repentance—a people to be given over to the mark of the beast. I really fear for this generation; their innocence is lost, and it's really not their

The Holiness of God

fault. There are prophecies that say that God is going to intervene and raise this generation up. I believe it is true.

I know that God is going to do something to break this cycle. Over the last few years, I've been going to a music festival called Creation Fest. It's mostly a bunch of Christian bands playing for a lot of Christian kids that have been camping out for several days.

It was a love-hate relationship for me. I was shocked at the kind of music that they listened to. But at the same time, it was so cool seeing everybody worshipping Jesus. It was still way better than any of the worldly concerts I've been to.

The first year I went, I was looking over all the camps, and I had the feeling of how Joshua felt looking over the children of Israel before going into the promised land. There were thousands of them. God told me to walk up and down the camps and listen to them and learn to love them. He said if I couldn't love them, then He would not receive my prayer for them. It only took just a little bit of walking, and my attitude changed. I just had to get over myself. I know that I'm not totally wrong in what I'm seeing, but God has got something germinating in them, and I've got to get out of the way and let Him do His thing.

The second year I went, He told me to walk up and down and pray over them. My mom died while I was there then, and that put me into a really deep place. When I walked, I felt like I was praying over them like Jesus prayed over

His disciples before He was crucified. That concert ended totally amazing. It was like creation itself was participating in it.

The third year I was there, we were all gathered together at a main event concert, and I was looking over the thousands of kids with their hands raised worshipping God, and God said to me, "This is My bride, and from now on I want you to bless her." So whatever it is that these kids have, it's going to be powerful.

God told me once that when Jesus comes in His people, He is coming from the bottom-up, not the top-down. Our kids are definitely on the bottom. They need a reverse whirlwind.

There is a lot more to this that I want to talk about later, but I want to show you another side about God, another side to the whirlwind, a reverse whirlwind. The Bible says that for some people, we persuade with the fear of the Lord, while with others, we persuade with the goodness of the Lord. My purpose above all is to show you Jesus, who He really is, and hopefully, if you are like me, you will want to fall in love with Him too and fear him.

Time and eternity coming together, what kind of a whirlwind is that going to create?

We see whirlwinds, tornadoes, hurricanes, etc. that destroy. When I looked up *whirlwind* in the concordance, all of its listings were in the Old Testament. I wonder if that means anything. Anyway, I see a good side to God's whirlwind. He takes things that are chaotic and destroyed, spins them back together, and brings wholeness and purpose out of it.

I can see this in my life so much. I think my most worst chaotic time was when the paperwork was getting done for my divorce. My wife and I had been separated for over three years, and neither one of us was getting it done. I couldn't, I just couldn't, accept that it was really happening. I can really understand the power of denial now.

Anyway, I was drinking myself to death. My probation officer told me to get out of town, and sober up, or she was going to throw me in jail. I called my dad, and he came and got me. At the same time, he decided he was going to file for my divorce, so I let him.

While I was at his house trying to get sober, I was weaning myself down too fast. The hospital there wouldn't give me Librium. Watching my dad filling out the divorce papers and going through alcohol withdrawal, it became too much for my brain to handle, and I went into a full-blown seizure. Luckily, my dad's wife was a retired nurse, and she got me through it. I didn't remember any of it when I woke up the next morning.

That seizure did something to my brain. Since then, sometimes I come to a place that my mind can't handle anymore, and I feel myself going into that anxiety shutdown mode. It's not a fun thing to go through.

I've been sober over eight years now, and I still have to control how much I think about, and also, I have to decide on what really is important to think about. I can still get overwhelmed and push myself over the edge.

When I first got sober, sometimes anxiety would hit me so hard at nights that I would literally roll out of bed on to the floor. Then I crawled on my belly to my stereo and turned on Christian worship music. I'd lay there until God's peace hit me, and that would bring me out of it. It works every time; I don't take any kind of prescription drugs. I know the power of God's peace, and if you've ever been in that place, you know what I mean.

It doesn't get that drastic anymore, but I can still overdo it from time to time. Sometimes it seems to come out of nowhere. God takes my chaos and brings order and peace to it, which is of great value to me. That is something nobody can tell me different. I was a shattered person, and God has been putting me back together since.

The Bible says that in the last days, men's hearts will fail them for fear of what's coming on the earth. So, even the best of people are going to need something to keep their minds from blowing apart. I see the whirlwind coming, both to destroy the works of the enemy and to restore the children of God.

Another thing I see is the Bible like a reverse black hole. Even though it has a beginning and an end, the knowledge that comes out of it is infinite, there is just no end to learning what is contained in those pages. This is proof to me, more than anything, that there is a God; and to think God lives in me, what a wonder. I have a birth and a death, but eternity is in me.

4

Believe

In this chapter, I'm going to tell the story about Lazarus being raised from the dead. I watch a movie called *The Gospel of John* a lot. I don't watch TV, but I don't get tired of this movie. It's like that reverse black hole I was talking about that you never stop learning from. I've been watching this movie off and on for over six years, and I still keep seeing new things. Things that don't make sense all of a sudden make sense and fit together. The story of Lazarus's resurrection was one of those stories.

I've been challenged by God to think for myself and listen for Him to teach me things. I'm not out to cause division. This you can take, or leave, or put on the shelf. But if I'm right, you will see Jesus, Mary, and Martha in a new light. It's just kind of fun. My main point of the story I think we will all agree on is about *believing*. It's probably the most important point of the Christian life. For the person new to Christianity, this will make the difference in how easy, or hard, it will be to bury your old nature and live in the new.

The story starts in Luke 10:38–42 (NKJV),

> Now it happened as they went that He entered a certain village; and a certain woman named Martha welcomed Him into her house. And she had a sister called Mary, who also sat at Jesus feet and heard His word. But Martha was distracted with much serving, and she approached Him and said, "Lord, do you not care that my sister has left me to serve alone? Therefore tell her to help me." And Jesus answered and said to her, "Martha, Martha, you are worried and troubled about many things. But one thing is needed, and Mary has chosen that good part, which will not be taken away from her."

Mary did well; she went against her hospitality tradition to listen to Jesus. Martha thought she was doing well by her works, but really, her fault was in her complaining. She found out that it was Jesus's words that were more important for life, not food. Did Martha become teachable? I believe she did. This part here is her failure, but later I say she becomes the true hero of the story, and Mary almost stumbles, but Jesus catches her and raises her up to an even higher place.

> Now a certain man was sick, Lazarus of Bethany, the town of Mary and her sister Martha. It was that Mary who anointed the Lord with fragrant oil and wiped His feet with her hair, whose brother Lazarus was sick. Therefore the sisters sent to Him, saying, "Lord, behold, he whom You love is sick." When Jesus heard

that, He said, "*This sickness is not unto death*, but for the glory of God, that the Son of God may be *glorified through it*." (John 11:1–4, NKJV)

Now the sisters sent word to Jesus, and I'm sure they were expecting word back from Him and that He was coming. But most importantly, Jesus said that this sickness was not going to be unto death. So the sisters had to be relieved that Jesus was coming to save the day: "Now Jesus loved Martha and her sister and Lazarus. So, when He heard that he was sick, He stayed two more days in the place where He was" (John 11:5–6).

Jesus loved the sisters, but He stayed and let Lazarus die. He wasn't very far away, and really, all He had to do was say the word and Lazarus would have been healed. Now what kind of love is this that would be going through the girls' minds? Especially when it sounded like He was coming to save the day? Wouldn't there be feelings of betrayal, and anger, and confusion, trying to make sense of it all? Sounds like a test to me. Has God ever put you in that kind of place?

> Then after this He said to the disciples, "Let us go to Judea again." The disciples said to Him, "Rabbi, lately the Jews sought to stone You, and are You going there again?" Jesus answered, "Are there not twelve hours in the day? If anyone walks in the day, he does not stumble, because he sees the light of this world. But if he walks in the night, he stumbles, because the light is not in him." (John 11:8–10)

They had just come from Judea, where twice the Jews wanted to stone Him. But Jesus was still after His people, so there's a second story going on here. He doesn't get rejected easily, and He doesn't give up on us.

> These things He said, and after that He said to them, "Our friend Lazarus sleeps, but I go that I may wake him up." Then His disciples said, "Lord, if he sleeps he will get well." However, Jesus spoke of his death, but they thought that He was speaking about taking rest in sleep. Then Jesus said to them plainly, "Lazarus is dead. And I am *glad* for your sakes that I was not there, *that you may believe*. Nevertheless let us go to him." Then Thomas, who is called the Twin, said to his fellow disciples, "Let us also go, *that we may die with Him*." (John 11:11–16; emphasis added)

This is the third story going on at the same time. Notice that Jesus said He was *glad* for their sakes so that they may *believe*. Well, the disciples were willing to die with Him, even Judas Iscariot, so how much more believing does He want? But they weren't seeing Him as going to the cross; they were seeing Him as becoming king and driving out Rome. They didn't understand His talk about Him dying. Jesus simply wants us to *believe* Him for what He says, not in our preconceived ideas about Him: "So when Jesus came, He found that he had been in the tomb four days. Now Bethany was near Jerusalem, about two miles away. And many of the Jews had joined the women around Martha

The Holiness of God

and Mary, to comfort them concerning their brother" (John 11:17–19).

Back in John 10:40, it says that Jesus was at a place beyond the Jordan, where John first baptized. John 1:28 says John baptized in Bethabara beyond the Jordan. By my map in the back of my Bible, I calculated that Bethabara was about sixteen miles from Bethany. I had to walk fifteen miles once, and I did it in about five hours.

If Jesus waited two days until Lazarus was dead, and Lazarus was in the grave four days when He showed up, then by my math, it took Jesus four days to walk roughly sixteen miles. That's four miles per day. He must have stopped and visited at every house and person on the way. Jesus couldn't do anything in secret, so it probably wasn't any secret that He was coming and taking His sweet time at that. I wonder what Martha and Mary were thinking by then?

> Then Martha, as soon as she heard that Jesus was coming, went and met Him, but Mary was sitting in the house. Now Martha said to Jesus, "*Lord*, if you had been here, my brother would not have died. But *even now* I know that *whatever You ask* of God, God will give You." Jesus said to her, "Your brother will rise again." Martha said to Him, "I know that he will rise again in the resurrection at the last day." (John 11:20–24; emphasis added)

This is where I say Martha is the true hero of the whole story. Martha was hurt and angry—this was a major thing—but she still called Him *Lord*. Jesus and His disciples had raised people from the dead before, so could it be that in the back of her mind she was daring to *believe* Jesus? That He was there to keep His word and raise Lazarus up, not letting this sickness be unto death? Is that what she meant when she said "whatever You ask"? I think she had hope, and that's what drove her out there to Him.

People don't always say what they mean, and you have to read them. What if that's what was happening with her, and Jesus knew the hope that was really in her heart? So He went right to the point and said, "Lazarus will rise again." It was easy for her to say that he would rise in the resurrection, which still fulfilled His word. But could she daresay what was really in her heart. I still can't help but think that she knew who she was really in the presence of. There is a reason why I say all of this, and I will show why in a few more verses: "Jesus said to her, 'I am the resurrection and the life. He who *believes* in Me, though he may die, he shall live. And whoever lives and *believes* in Me shall never die. Do you *believe* this?' She said to Him, 'Yes, Lord, *I believe that You are the Christ, the Son of God*, who is to come into the world'" (John 11:25–27; emphasis added).

Now Jesus fully reveals Himself, and she *believed* Him. She passed the test with a well-done.

> And when she had said these things, she went her way and secretly called Mary her sister, saying, "The Teacher has come and is calling for you." As soon as she heard that, she arose quickly and came to Him. Now Jesus had not yet come into town, but was in the place where Martha met Him. Then the Jews who were with her in the house, and comforting her, when they saw that Mary rose up quickly and went out, followed her, saying, "She is going to the tomb to weep there." (John 11:28–31)

I often wonder why Mary stayed in the house when Martha left the first time. Was she angry, or did she not know Jesus was there? Notice that Jesus stayed outside the city instead of going into town to meet with her. Would she be angry and just stay away? Nope, she went, and that's a picture for us, even if we are angry. How often do we feel God at a distance, and do we press in to find Him? He is always calling to us.

> Then when Mary came where Jesus was, and saw Him, she *fell down at His feet*, saying to Him, "*Lord*, if You had been here, my brother would not have died." Therefore, when Jesus saw her weeping, and the Jews who came with her weeping, He *groaned* in spirit and was *troubled*. And He said, "Where have you laid him?" They said to Him, "*Lord*, come and see." *Jesus wept*. Then the Jews said, "See how He loved him." (John 11:32–36; emphasis added)

These are the main verses I wanted to come to in the whole story. I had seen something in Jesus that brought tears to my eyes. When we read this, I think we get misled by the Jews when they said, "See how He loved him." And we think Jesus wept for Lazarus, but I think it was different.

Jesus loved Lazarus, Martha, and Mary. This was their test. Not just to expose where they were at, but to make them grow to an even higher place in Him. And, eventually, they passed all the way. This is our story too.

Poor Lazarus, he got sick and let die. To me, it was more than just coincidence. Jesus was using him to bring light to a nation, and ultimately to us. A physical death and resurrection in this life, can you imagine Lazarus's relationship with Jesus after he was raised?

Now it's Mary's turn. She knew Jesus. She knew that He was not out to cruelly hurt them. So He must have had a reason for not saving Lazarus, but she was hurt and didn't understand. When she came to Him, she fell at His feet and called Him Lord. She didn't cuss Him out and chase Him off. But she didn't go as far as Martha did and dared to *believe*. She passed the test, not completely, but eventually; she did make it to where Jesus wanted her to be.

Jesus wants us to call Him Lord and Teacher because it is right, but even more—He wants us to *believe* Him. When Mary and the Jews came weeping, Jesus *groaned* in spirit and was troubled. That word *groan* in the Greek is a word of anger, with a deep feeling of admonishment. Jesus wasn't happy with them because they didn't *believe* Him. I believe He *wept* over them because of the hardness of their hearts. I believe the Jews misread Him when they thought He was weeping for Lazarus because they didn't know Him.

It would be like you sitting in your apartment crying because you can't pay your rent, and you're getting evicted to the streets. I decide to save your day and go over to give you a check to pay your rent off. When I get to your house, I'm not going to cry with you when I know that I have your check in my back pocket. But it would make me feel bad if you wouldn't *believe* me that I was there to help. And remember, Jesus let Lazarus die, if at any time He would have cried, it would have been then. But instead, He was "glad for their sakes." I'm not saying Jesus was heartless, but He was a soldier doing His job, knowing the end from the beginning: "And some of them said, 'Could not this Man, who opened the eyes of the blind, also have kept this man from dying?' Then Jesus, again *groaning* in Himself, came to the tomb. It was a cave, and a stone lay against it" (John 11:37–38; emphasis added).

They had just witnessed Jesus healing the blind man with the mud that He had put on his eyes in Jerusalem. Would it have been any harder for them to have said "He healed the blind man, couldn't He also raise up Lazarus?" He had raised the dead before, but I'm sure that because they weren't dead long enough, people began saying that the dead person wasn't really totally dead. They had a belief that a dead person's spirit hung around for three days, and when their body started decomposing then they left—the hardness of their hearts to *believe*. So now, with Lazarus, they knew he was dead: "Jesus said, 'Take away the stone.' Martha, the sister of him who was dead, said to Him, 'Lord, by this time there is a stench, for he has been dead four days.' Jesus said to her, 'Did I not say to you that if you would *believe* you would see the glory of God?'" (John 11: 39–40; emphasis added).

I wonder if Jesus said "Take away the stone," He wasn't really praying, "Take away the stone from their hearts"? I pray that God would take away the stone from my heart and help me to *believe*.

Then Martha was reminding Him that it's been four days, and he's stinking by now. I think she's looking at the waves, like Peter, and the impossible is facing her, and her doubt is swaying her faith. But it's in Jesus's statement here, when He said, "Did I not say that if you would *believe*" that He was addressing her *believing* for Lazarus's resurrection now. Then she came into agreement with Him and allowed them to take away the stone.

> Then they took away the stone from the place where the dead man was lying. And Jesus lifted up His eyes and said, "Father, I thank you that You heard Me. And I know that You always hear Me, but because of the people who are standing by I said this, that they may *believe* that you sent Me." Now when He had said

> these things, He cried with a loud voice, "Lazarus, come forth!" And he who had died came out bound hand and foot with grave clothes, and his face was wrapped in cloth. Jesus said to them, "Loose him and let him go."…Then, from that day on, they (the Jews) plotted to put Him to death. (John 11:41–44, 53; emphasis added)

From the very beginning, Jesus said this sickness was not unto death. That's why He said in His prayer, "I thank You that You heard Me." And when He said, "Because of the people who are standing by I said this." It meant that they knew He had said that this was not unto death. He was after them to get them to *believe*. Then He raised Lazarus up.

Some who *believed* went to the Jews, but the Jews plotted to kill Him. Now, instead of the test taking those ones to a higher place in God, they became worse and wanted to kill God. It's almost like that dividing line that I talked about earlier. But Mary does come through later and makes His day.

> Then six days before the Passover, Jesus came to Bethany, where Lazarus was who had been dead, whom He had raised from the dead. There they made Him a supper; *and Martha served*, but Lazarus was one of those who sat at the table with Him. Then Mary took a pound of very costly oil of spikenard, anointed the feet of Jesus, and wiped His feet with her hair.

> And the house was filled with the fragrance of the oil. But one of His disciples, Judas Iscariot, Simon's son, who would betray Him, said, "Why was this fragrant oil not sold for three hundred denarii and given to the poor?" This He said, not that he cared for the poor, but because he was a thief, and had the money box; and he used to take what was put in it. But Jesus said, "Let her alone; *she has kept this for the day of My burial.* For the poor you have with you always, but Me you do not have always." (John 12:1–8; emphasis added)

Jesus had already been telling them that He was going to die. But the disciples couldn't understand this and *believe* Him. They were looking for Him to become king. But Mary *believed* Him and anointed Him for His burial. She learned to take Him at His word. She passed the test, and she came to be remembered for it. And notice, Martha still served, but she didn't complain and was never rebuked for it.

I heard different preachings after I wrote this, and they really seemed to tear Martha down like she failed through the whole story, so finally I went for a walk, asking God if I'm wrong in what I'm seeing and if I should go back and delete all of this. I was really searching, and then it was like I was seeing a vision in my spirit, not my imagination, and I was standing before the courtroom of heaven, and all the people in heaven were there.

I was being judged for this story, and Martha walked out of the crowd of people and came up to me and gave me a great big hug in front of them all because for centuries people have discredited her, and I was one of the few who defended her honor. That hug became my badge of honor that all of the host of heaven would remember for the rest of eternity. It also showed me that we need to watch what we say, even of the people that have passed on, because one day we will meet them, and they will know. So I'm keeping the story.

5

Old Man *(Nature)*, Die!

Last night, I had a dream that I was in the bars getting drunk with my friends. Even after eight years of being sober, once in a great while, I will have a dream about drinking. At the end of this dream, I didn't want to be a drunk anymore, but I was so bound up by it. I began to pray, and I asked God to "put flesh on His Spirit." Then I started to wake up, and I realized I was free from drugs and alcohol, and that I had been free for a long time. That felt so good.

I believe that God was showing me that over the years, He has been aligning my flesh to His Spirit that He put in me. I could see the difference so clearly. All my other times of sobriety were not like this one. I had almost eight years of sobriety before and relapsed, but this time, it is so different.

Before, I did start out good at being a Christian, but eventually it became a mask. I knew how to look like one, but inside I was falling apart. This time, I am doing better. I believe this is what I am supposed to talk about. I had three dreams right in a row the other night, and it was like God was saying, *It's time to start writing again.*

I won't tell all three dreams right now, but I will start with the first one. In my dream, I was in charge of a cemetery. I put people in coffins and buried them. It was weird though, I wasn't burying their physical bodies. I was rolling them up in a mat that was just wider than them, and when I would roll the dead person up, it just looked like a rolled-up mat.

I had a helper, and I was teaching him how to bury a body the right way versus doing it the wrong way. I could get about six people who were rolled up in mats in one coffin before I would have to bury the coffin.

I was teaching my helper how to prepare the bodies the "clean way" so that they would not stink after a while. That was important because when we had to take the lid off the coffin to put the next body in that death smell could get pretty bad. We had two bodies to put into the coffins. We pulled the lid off the one coffin and threw one of the bodies in. It went pretty well; the death smell was very minimal.

The second body we had to put in another coffin was one that I wasn't in charge of. So we took it over to the other coffin, and I told the guy in charge that we had to put this body in his coffin. He was almost like a scary person with occult powers. He stayed in the shadows; it was at night, under the light of the moon. He said okay, and with his powers, he lifted the lid off the coffin by itself.

I told my helper that this guy's way was the bad way to bury someone, that we needed to hurry, throw this body in, and not get too close. We tossed the body in, but the smell

The Holiness of God

of death was so bad that it woke me up. When I woke up, I had the smell of death so bad in my nose that I had to get up. It took a while for that smell to go away, and then I wondered what this dream was all about.

I went back to bed and had two more dreams that had death in them. That morning, I got up and had to go for a walk to shake them off; they were so real. Later, I did figure out that they were God's dreams, so I took them serious. They were like a kick in the pants for me to get writing again.

I believe that God is telling me to teach people that there is a clean way to put to death our old natures, and that there is an ugly way to put to death our old natures. I've been through both, and the ugly way is not very fun.

There are no deep secrets to this. Most of this is so simple even a child could understand. It seems that we are the ones who make it hard. As Christians, we do a physical baptism to represent what we do spiritually. But even though it sounds easy, for some of us, it's not as easy as it looks.

You know, when you are sitting in jail looking at going to prison because you drink too much, you should start thinking that it's time to get this figured out. It's better to be sober and able to be free at home than to be sober in jail. The fear of death didn't stop me, but life in jail somehow didn't seem worth it.

So I know that I can never drink or use again, and I don't have any more chances. I have no more room to fail.

Obviously, I'm not perfect, but if I let my old man live, I'm dead.

When I first got sober, I was in such a deep depression. I never smiled. The rehab counselor, drug court people, and the psychologist they sent me to all wanted to put me on antidepressants. I can't take antidepressants; it's like I smoked a joint and never came down. Plus that seizure feeling and claustrophobia would come on me, and I finally just had to say, "No more."

I had to learn how to walk out of depression on my own, and it wasn't easy. But within a year, I was smiling again. Mostly, I learned that I had to talk about what I really felt, no matter how foolish it made me look. Then I came to find that many people were feeling the same way I did. So then, I realized that I'm not so unique and irreparable after all.

I had to do a lot of recovery meetings then, sometimes four a day, plus all the drug court meetings. That's what I had to do to stay sober that first year especially. Sometimes, I would go to church, but then end up going to a meeting just to recover from church. I had a hard time with church.

Then, after two years of being sober, recovery meetings weren't doing it for me anymore, and there was a moment that I did become willing to drink again. So I had to do something different. I talked a lot about that in book one.

One thing I learned was that it was no different for me to quit drinking at forty-three as it would have been when I was seventeen. I still had to say no, and I still had to overcome. The only difference was, the older I got, the harder it was to say no. Plus, true freedom isn't in just saying no while at the same time you still want to drink. True freedom is when the desire is gone, and you can move on to do something else.

Right now, I'm using alcoholism as an example. I learned this too when I quit smoking cigarettes. Cigarette was hard, I had to use the patch to quit. I'd quit, and then a few years later, I'd start back up again and then quit again. It was total misery, but then the power it had over me was broken, and I've never craved one since, which has been about thirteen years now. I saw that my new man was growing, and that it had become stronger than my old man in that area.

I believe it happens in every area of our lives that something has a hold of us in, and it takes our new man to grow up strong enough to conquer it. And once it's conquered, you don't fall for it anymore; you are free from it as long as you keep the old man dead. Then you have to start learning boundaries.

The key is in *believing*. In the beginning, I wrestled with this. I thought it was just a psychological mind game and retraining our old nature. But God said that He made us a new creation, and that old things are passed away. When we are born again, we really can find that new person inside of us, and we can grow into who that new person is.

Some people grow fast, and some slow. It all depends on how bad you want to let go of the old. It's a growing process. That's where a new believer needs to be mentored by people who are willing to take the time it takes to grow. The Holy Spirit is ultimately our lifelong mentor.

There are scriptures in the Bible that talk of "No one builds a house without first sitting down and making sure that they have enough money," or "No one goes to war without examining their army to see if they are strong enough to win," or "Sets his hand to a plow, and looks back."

Well, I'm probably one of them, dumb ones, but I didn't want to go to hell, and the life I was living wasn't worth gambling my eternity for. So I had to keep trying to become a Christian, even if I didn't have what it took to do it. I always fell short and looked back. To me, I was like Peter getting out of the boat and trying to walk on water. I sank a lot. But God saved me, and He helped teach me how to walk in His strength.

For the last few years, in the spring, I've had to battle with allergies. I actually get high on the air I breathe. Then the air becomes like sandpaper and makes my sinuses feel like hamburger. I have to take allergy pills, sometimes several times a day, and after a while I start feeling just like I'm on meth. It wakes my old man up, then after the seasons over, it usually takes a few months for me to get back to being me again.

It's like I've had to rehearse putting my old man down every year. This last year was particularly hard. One of my old time best friends moved away and went back to his old

The Holiness of God

ways. It hurt. I'm still not good at handling pain. It seemed like a rerun of the last time I was eight years sober, when my wife left me and went back to her old ways.

I felt like it was a test. Would I go back to my old ways? Plus, after being doped up like on meth made life hard. It was a battle between my old man and new. All those close times I had with God felt gone, but He still showed me that He was there every day. And that's when having Christian friends becomes important too.

How do we put to death our old man? The Bible says that we are to *reckon* ourselves dead, like baptism. It sounds simple, but again, you really have to *believe* that there really is power from God that is supernaturally changing you when you do this. It's not a mind game. The proof is in gaining total freedom from your bondage and not wanting it anymore. Sometimes it's a long process, but when it breaks, you know it, and it's gone. You don't have to spend the rest of your life fighting it.

A lot of things just die away from us by the Spirit of God, and we don't have to do anything. We just change. The old ways become death to us; if it's not good for us, then we don't want to do it anymore. It's hard to explain, but that happens. Old friends eventually don't want to be around us because we are different now.

Sometimes it's hard. When you're growing into a new world, doing new things, battling life, you get wore out, but you just have to keep *believing*. Eventually, God does come through and renews our strength, and things change. It's like spiritual weightlifting. It develops strength and character in us if we don't give up.

Going back to the old man can be real subtle too. I've always had this prophetic thing in me that I've kept to myself. When I would go to church, that voice would activate in me, and it would almost become like I was drunk. I would start telling people what I believed God was telling me to tell them. Then after I got home, it would be like I'd sober up, and I'd say, "Oh no, what did I just do?"

Then I'd go back to work and be with my old friends to get back to reality. Then I'd stay away from church for a while. It's really hard to keep the old man dead when you're still tied to the old world. Eventually, I would go back to church, and then that same thing would happen again. Every time I got around them, that thing would activate in me.

It's still not easy for me, but I've had to accept that's what God put in me, and that's what I have to develop. It's not enough anymore to just sit in the back row and not be a part of the body.

Another thing I've learned too is if you live in the old man, you still live under the old curse. Things you did in the past, and generational curses, are only broken when you walk in the new man, cleansed by the blood of Jesus.

I believe as well that the anointing for overcoming that's helped me can come on you by you reading this book. In fact, this is the word that was given to me in the beginning. It comes from Isaiah 45:2–3, 52:12, and 55:6–13. I put it together, and this is what it says:

> Seek the Lord while He may be found, call upon Him while He is near. Let the wicked forsake his way, and the unrighteous man his thoughts; Let him return to the Lord, and He will have mercy on him; and to our God, for He will abundantly pardon. "For My thoughts are not your thoughts, nor are your ways My ways," says the Lord. "For as the heavens are higher than the earth, so are My ways higher than your ways, and My thoughts than your thoughts. For as the rain comes down, and the snow from heaven, and do not return there, but water the earth, and make it bring forth and bud, that it may give seed to the sower and bread to the eater, so shall My word be that goes forth from My mouth; it shall not return to me void, but it shall accomplish what I please, and it shall prosper in the thing for which I sent it. I will go before you and make the crooked places straight; I will break in pieces the gates of bronze and cut the bars of iron. I will give you treasures of darkness and hidden riches of secret places, that you may know that I, the Lord, who call you by your name, am the God of Israel. For you shall not go out with haste, nor go by flight. For the Lord will go before you, and the God of Israel will be your rear guard. For you shall go out with joy, and be led out with peace; the mountains and the hills shall break forth into singing before you, and all the

trees of the field shall clap their hands. Instead of the thorn shall come up the cypress tree, and instead of the brier shall come up the myrtle tree; and it shall be to the Lord for a name, for an everlasting sign that shall not be cut off."

6

New Man, Live!

After receiving Jesus as our personal Lord and Savior, we are told to get baptized. This is a baptism of our flesh where we get dunked in water. It symbolizes that we are repenting from living for ourselves to living for God, dying into Jesus's death and raising into His resurrection.

Then there is a baptism in our spirit. The Holy Spirit unites to our spirit and births us into God's kingdom. This is where our new man draws its power from, to overcome our old mind-set nature that we had been used to living in.

Our physical body changes when we die, and we get a new one in the resurrection. We have to overcome our old thinking with our new thinking, and our spirits are made new now. Our new man draws us toward God, and our old man pushes us away from God. It's that simple. Our worst enemy is our battle between the two. If there is a deep secret in God, it is this: Jesus baptizes us with His Spirit and makes us His brothers and sisters into the family of God. And all are welcomed!

God is real, He is a person, and He wants a personal relationship with us now, not just after we die and get to heaven. It's in our new man that we see and hear Him. And we all can see and hear from Him ourselves. But it comes from spending time with Him and developing a relationship with Him.

These last eight years of being sober is where I've really learned to develop a relationship with God. When I talked earlier about trying to become a Christian after I first got saved, it was more a figure of speech. I was always still saved because I am living as a Christian now. But if I would have died while I was living in my old backslidden world, I don't know for sure where I'd be. There are no guarantees when you go back to the old life. You only know you're okay if you make it back to the new one.

I feel like God wants me to tell you about my life now. I'm thinking, *Are you sure, God?* I have no great story to tell. I had a visitation from God about six years ago, and that changed me, but the memory of that had faded. It's what I've developed with God since then that keeps me going now, and that's what I need to talk about.

I live in a basement apartment that once was a basement house. It used to be our storage place for keeping materials for the other apartments we worked on. That was back when I was married. Then, my wife wanted to separate for three months, so I talked my landlord into letting me fix this place up to live in for that three months. I've been here now over thirteen years.

The Holiness of God

In the beginning it was just concrete floors, concrete walls, little windows, the ceiling is about six feet high, and my toilet and shower are in the same room, separated by a shower curtain. After I got out of jail, this place felt no different than my jail cell.

Now it's been affectionately named the man cave. It reminds me of King David when he had to live in a cave while Saul was after him. It's fixed up pretty good now, so it is a nice cave to live in. But I will be glad when I can move. It seems like God planted me here, it's like He stuck me here so that me and Him could develop a relationship together.

I live next to a park that I walk around a lot when this place gets too lonely. I used to call the park my "green mile." The *green mile* was a term used for the distance from a jail cell to the electric chair. It is a nice park; this whole setup is nice when I stop whining. I don't even like living in this city. I like small towns and the country. I'm always begging God to move, but the answer has always been No. So, I'm learning to be thankful for where I'm at and what I have. Besides, if it wasn't for God, I could be in hell right now.

I wouldn't trade any of this for any place in the world if it's without God. I know someday He will say it's time I can go, but until then. I do really enjoy what I have with God here; take that away, and you might as well put me in the grave. But how do you tell people about it?

Right now, it's a hard time for me. Three families in my Christian circle have lost a child to car accidents in the last few months. Curtis, who I wrote about in Book One, lost his daughter in a wreck about a month ago. The gal, whose word I wrote in Book One, got hit almost head-on a couple of days ago, and her youngest son was lost. A couple in our church who are elders lost their son in a wreck a few months ago. Another elder lost his son earlier too in a motorcycle wreck, and we are saying, What is going on here?

Before I started writing this book, I had felt this intense need to pray, but I didn't know what to pray for. I just sensed that God was telling me that He was getting ready to do something really good in the church. That this was our time of His visitation, to not miss it, and that we are now in the new day. I basically finished what I had as far as work and started praying.

I prayed like all day and into a week, and then a week turned into a few weeks. In the meantime, after going to two funerals, it sure didn't feel like something good was happening. But we don't see things with how God sees them. It's in times like this that we just have to keep trusting God. We question if we're doing anything wrong, but I know that's not the problem. If anything, I believe we are doing something right even though we're not perfect. So we are praying. We don't want to lose any more kids.

Right now, it's like what I wrote in the first paragraph of this book: where Jesus is saying, "My God, My God, why have You forsaken me…But you are holy, enthroned in the praises of Israel." That's where real growth is, it's trusting and praising God even though life hurts.

That's the place where I had to come to in the beginning to stay alive, especially after I first got out of jail. I hurt and craved alcohol bad, but I made it through. What I thought I could never heal from, God turned into something positive, and I'm becoming a better person for it. That old saying is true that says, "I never want to go through that again, but now that it's over, I'm glad I went through it." I'm not saying this about losing a child, that is bad; we have to trust God that He is going to bring good out of it.

My life isn't like moving out from following one set of rules to following another and waiting for the benefits, even though that is true. There are benefits from following God's rules—true—but it is His presence, feeling Him in my life. It's like what to a couple who wants a relationship to each other where all they can do is send letters to each other. It's that personal contact that makes a relationship work. It's the same with God.

Sometimes, I feel Him at a distance, especially if I'm in my old man. But there are times that His presence is so strong that when I have to come back to this world's reality, it's like I might as well be going to the dark side of the moon. He's what makes life for me. That's where the new man can go with God, and it is available for everybody.

I also learned this back when my world was so bad that I was on my knees bawling, embarrassing to talk about now, but God came and His presence lifted me completely above all my problems. There was so much peace and love that I forgot about my life and could care less if I had another girl again.

In fact, I get to a place of having seasons with God where I could go the rest of my life without having a woman in my life. Then it happens I see one, and I get all messed up. I'm not into making myself a eunuch or celibate, but it does create a war in me. It's that kind of presence with God that makes life worth living.

He doesn't just let me experience that presence with Him all the time. I think because of me being an alcoholic, I could abuse His presence like a drug and not be in it for Him. In the beginning, He controlled it, but the more I choose Him and His ways over mine, the more His presence is there. That's just the beginning of a whole new life with God.

Then it becomes learning how to wait. There is no formula. It changes all the time. Most of the time, I can get into His presence through worship music. A real deep place comes when I've been in that after a few hours. To me, it's like climbing a mountain. It takes work to get all the problems out of my mind until I finally become totally focused on Him. It's when you see Him that you become like Him.

Then I come into a place where I pray for people who come into my mind. There are times I can be in that abandoned place for hours and hours. I basically developed it because I have nowhere else to go, and I have nothing but time. That is one benefit of being in my cave.

I don't expect people to live like me, but I can't see how people can live not like me. It seems to me that there is an agenda in this world that is slowly destroying people. Turning to God and being within His boundaries is the only way we are going to make it.

Jesus said that we are to worship God in spirit and in truth. The Bible also says to put on the belt of truth. Righteousness and justice are what we are to align ourselves to, and we learn this from reading the Bible. God also says that when we receive Him, He writes His laws in our hearts, our new man.

This means that we aren't forced to live by His rules; we *want* to live by His rules.

I can't stress enough the importance of reading your Bible and learning to think for yourself. I see the Bible like a belt. It starts with page one, the buckle, and ends with the last page, the tip of the belt. After you are done reading the whole Bible, then start over again. It's like buckling up your belt around your waist. Usually, I read the Old Testament once, then the New Testament a couple of times, and then I start over again.

It's important to get to know the whole Bible. That's where we draw from to renew our mind and gain right thinking. Some places don't have the Bible, but we do.

And get into fellowship. We need to be around people who love God and have right thinking. Sometimes, that's a challenge. I have found in most churches that I've been to there is at least a core group who are really serious about God. And trust your heart: if God is telling you that something is wrong, get out.

7

Indians to the Rescue

I had a dream last night. Somehow I think it has to do with everything that's been happening here lately. It started out that I was doing some work. A judge and his son whom I know were helping me carry some tools from his house to where I was working. I had been working on the judge's house, but now I was working across the street trying to hang a door, and my dad was there. My dad kept hanging on me, and it was hindering me from getting this door hung, so I was struggling.

Next, a lady preacher that I know who preaches all around the world came up to me. She said that she had a job for me. In this dream, she was like Oprah Winfrey; she was very wealthy with a lot of clout. She wanted me to go to this town, which I believe was my old hometown; we had that place in common. She wanted me to take my tools and go help these people there. She was going to finance the whole thing, so I said okay, and I went there.

Once I got there, I stopped at a place to eat. I was sitting at a table, and there was somebody I knew sitting across from me and my former probation officer beside me. There was something about the food that was wrong, so I left.

I went and found where I was supposed to go. It was a whole community of Indians living in one great big barn. I introduced myself and told them why I was there. They started showing me around and showing me the things that they were doing. Most of it was like entertainment; it was really good, highly skilled, and awe-inspiring but had little value. It wasn't work, building things, and making a living. Then we decided to call a meeting.

We all gathered in the open area of the barn. Now it was night; it was a warm summer night, so they had all the doors and windows open. The windows were just shutters that you opened out, there was no glass. I was sitting next to the chief, and he was telling me that occasionally there was a sniper outside, and he would shoot someone inside and kill them to disrupt their meetings. I asked him why they didn't close everything up so that they couldn't be seen.

He said that they were Christians, and that they weren't going to hide, even if it meant their life. It reminded me of the scriptures that talk about not hiding our light. So I understood. All the men there had their shirts off; it was their custom, so I had my shirt off too. Then the thought hit me that I am really white, and I will stand out. If there was a sniper out there, I could easily be picked off, but I got brave and joined in.

The Holiness of God

I found out that the whole city there was against them, even the police wouldn't help. They could not buy food or anything else and were limited only to that barn. It was like the white men wanted them dead. The only way they could survive was by going to the river and finding food, which they became really good at. They had to survive on their own or die.

Then morning came, and all of a sudden it was like all of the people of the whole city was there outside. They shut all of our doors and windows and had us trapped inside. I thought, *Boy, what did I get into now?* I figured we were dead. I could hear the word *fire* being used outside, so I thought the people of the city were going to burn us down and kill us all. I could hear a lot of heavy equipment outside, and I figured they were going to haul our ashes off when they were done.

I asked the chief about calling the police, but he said it was no good, and then I realized that I had left my phone out in the car. So I thought this was it, this is how I was going to die. I was looking at the roof waiting for the fire and smoke, and wondering how this could really be happening. I had never seen racial tension like this before.

Then it all went quiet. All the noise outside was gone, so we looked out to see what was happening. It turned out that there was a big fire in the main part of town. There was a warehouse on the other side of us that had the entire city's heavy equipment in, and they were rushing the equipment over to put out the fire. For some reason, they were just being courteous to us by closing our doors to keep the dust that they were creating from blowing in on us.

In the end, the fire destroyed everything. The city had no more food, and all means of livelihood was gone. There was nothing left, and now they were going to die. But the Indians had compassion—they were Christians—and because they were forced to survive off the river, they knew how to get food and so they went and brought it to the city people. Then they were all grateful.

The food was bird eggs that they got off the river banks, and they harvested something out of the river that they made something like peanut butter. It was really good and really high in nutrition. Now everybody became friends. Then I realized that I was the only one with power tools, and that now it was my job to help rebuild the whole town. Then I woke up.

There's a lot to this dream, but for now I want to focus on the Indians. Indians are the true Native Americans; they are connected to this land. To me, they represent the wholehearted Christians who are firmly grounded in God. In every church that I've been to, there's been a core group that is truly dedicated to God. They have a heart for each other, and they show up for everything.

They press in to find the deeper things of God and often find themselves alienated from the rest of the church. They have an openness to each other, *represented by the men not wearing their shirts*, that creates a family atmosphere, where all are allowed to participate.

The tendency is to become ingrown because they are not allowed to reach out to offer the life of the One whom they have found. They get attacked by word curses from people who know not what they say, and it does damage. Word curses happen when we render judgments on people, including ourselves, which God hasn't. But God is finding favor for His remnant and is sending help.

I'm going to write about favor in my next chapter. I'm calling it "The Favor of Esther." I believe there is coming to the church a holy fire. I don't know what it is going to look like, even though I think God has given me glimpses, but it is going to disrupt the old security of the church as a whole.

The people who have been forced to draw life from the river of God will then become the saving graces of the day. I was at work the other day, and I was pulling up some old carpet, and I found a marble. It had the colors in it of those bird eggs, white and blue rolling together into a pattern, like the ones the Indians got from the river, and it made me think again of that dream. I saved it and put it in my little God Box.

Then I noticed my journal that I take notes in when something inspires me to want to write about in my books. It had those same rolling colors in it, and it was like a lightbulb turned on. What if the day comes when we will no longer be allowed to have Bibles? What if the only inspired Word left to have is what people wrote in their journals. So those of you that keep journals, think about that. They just might become life for someone someday.

Then the denominational walls will come down. God is out to save His whole church; He has new wine coming and old wineskins to deal with. Blessed are those who have allowed God to make them into new wineskins now.

I had a dream once that I was standing on a grid, like grid paper. It was as if my life was being measured. I was proud because I could see all of my accomplishments, and I was doing well.

Then, all of a sudden, a big shaking happened. Now I found myself standing at another place on the grid paper, and this time the grid was three-dimensional. Now all of my little sins came up, and they were just as powerful at pulling me away from God as my big ones were. It was like an alcoholic drinking that first beer, thinking that it was okay, but it pulled me back anyway. How we see things and how God sees things are two different things.

When I woke up this is what I wrote: "A shaking is getting ready to happen. Where we think we are is not going to be where we really are. The question is will we be able to stand? All of our false paradigms will be gone. We have to press into Jesus now more than ever.

"The truth about us will be brought to the surface. We need to allow Him to prune us now. We have a false perception of grace. We think we are allowed little sins because we are only human, but we deceive ourselves. We need to get real and wake up. False grace is getting removed. Everything is going to get moved out of its place. We have to pay attention to the John the Baptists who are rising up."

God is so full of love, and He does love those who won't love Him back, so I'm not trying to put this heavy thing on people. But I think that there is something coming that is so terrible that it is going to bring out the worst in us, so I figure it is better to get dealt with now so that we can be strong when it happens.

At the same time, whatever it is that is going to happen is going to be so good that all of our little sins will become hindrances that keep us from coming into the fullness of what is happening. Wouldn't it be good to get rid of them now? I think both are going to happen at the same time. I think we have the greater responsibility, we have the Holy Spirit, we have the Bible, and we have freedom. We really have no excuses.

I told you we have had several deaths lately, and we've been questioning if this is more than just coincidence. We just had the little boy's funeral when at the same time we had already planned for a Burn (a twenty four-hour praise service). It was our first Burn since the one we had two years ago, where I first got the word to write these books. We went ahead and had the praise service, stopped for the funeral, and then finished after it.

During the Burn, several churches came together, and we sought God as to what was going on. The most common thing that came in from people all over the country who didn't know each other was word curses.

Word curses are just the tip of the iceberg or, actually, like the mouth of a volcano. The lava that flows out shows what's really inside. The words we say show what's in our hearts and, therefore, expose what's underneath.

To me, word curses sounded like a stretch for people to be getting killed over them. I didn't know what to think at the time, but I went with it. Then I believe I got a revelation. Here's another little Bible study in my words.

Remember King David. He had an affair with another man's wife, and she got pregnant. So he had the man killed and married the wife to hide all that he had done. But God revealed what he had done to the Prophet Nathan, and Nathan went and confronted David about it. Then Nathan pronounced a curse on him. He said in Samuel 12:10 (NKJV), "Now therefore, the sword shall *never* depart from your house, because you have despised Me" (emphasis added). Then death came to David's family—his son murdered his other son as well and also wanted to kill him too.

Then the curse passed down his family tree with murders and wars, and even his descendant King Josiah, whom the Bible says in 2 Kings 23:25 (NKJV): "Now before him there was no king like him, who turned to the Lord with all his soul, and with all his might, according to all the law of

The Holiness of God

Moses; nor after him did any arise like him." But, in the end, Josiah got killed in battle. The curse got him. Then there was a couple more kings after him, and then they went into captivity.

So what happened to the curse? Now we can read in the Gospels that Jesus is a direct descendant of King David; in fact, from what I've heard, Jesus by birthright would have been king. So did Jesus come under that curse?

Well according to this scripture, I say yes. Zechariah 13:7 (NKJV) says, "Awake O sword, against My Shepherd, against the Man who is My Companion," Says the Lord of hosts. "Strike the Shepherd and the sheep will be scattered." I believe Jesus was under that curse, and the devil used that as leverage against Him, but Jesus took that curse to the cross.

But the story doesn't end there. Now we go to the garden of Gethsemane on the night Jesus was betrayed. The Jews came to arrest Jesus, but Peter pulled out a sword to fight Jesus's arrest and cut off the ear of the servant of the high priest. Then Jesus told Peter to put down the sword; He said," All who live by the sword will die by the sword." Then Peter put down his sword, and Jesus healed the man's ear.

I believe this is all prophetic of us. When we become a Christian, we come into Jesus's lineage, and therefore, we come under that curse. But Jesus took that curse to the cross as long as we don't pick that sword back up. If we pick it back up and live by it, then we go back under that curse and will die by it. There is scripture after scripture telling us to beware of our tongue, and that it is a sword. I don't think I have to go into a lot of detail about that. You should already know.

So, could that be a reason why our families are falling apart and our churches are breaking up and even manifesting in deaths of people we love, and why people won't hear us anymore? Because we brought ourselves under a curse by criticizing each other so much?

The bright side is that when Peter put down the sword, Jesus healed the man's ear, telling me that if we repent, Jesus will heal the damage we caused, and people will hear us again. They will know us by our love.

I don't know everything. I have an idea of why word curses can now be even more powerful, and I will write about that in a later chapter. I think this chapter is more about relaying a message. I can tell you what we did at the Burn I believe we got God's judgment for our favor. We repented for us and for the church as a whole. We can't keep other people from cursing us, but we can keep from cursing other people.

I know this is an area that I need to work on too. I get so baffled at why people don't believe the same way I do. And I am so guarded against those who don't and even more guarded against those that I don't know. It's like you are guilty until you prove yourself innocent. I'm not supposed to be that way.

The Holiness of God

It seems like what God has been working on me now is to open up and allow other people to come into my life, even those I don't agree with all the time. Sometimes it gets hard to not judge them, but I'm finding that they have things that I need, and they do have a purpose in my life.

I want to end this chapter with a word that I believe God gave me for a lady in my church circle. I live next to an Indian reservation that she belongs to, and she has a deep cry for her people that I believe God honors. I think my dream is figurative and literal as well with the Native Americans.

It reads:

Mother of a Nation

I see this big black tree, old and gnarled up like you would see in a witch's tale. The tree is alive, but there is no life in it—there's no leaves or buds, just black branches. Then this tree starts swelling up like something inside is breaking out. The black bark begins cracking and splitting, and a green tree begins to break through. As the green tree breaks through, the black bark falls off like something shedding its skin. The tree branches then grow leaves and blossoms. The tree that once was dead is now a tree of life.

God tells me that this is what is happening in the Spirit realm when you pray. This tree is your family tree, and you are like inside this tree, bringing the transforming light that creates new life. But God is also birthing a nation through you. This deep travail that you have is the Holy

Spirit overshadowing you and conceiving through you new life into your family and nation. The Indian Nation will rise up again and be a great people, and you are a mother in this. Leaders will come out of your nation, leaders of governments, judges, and even one day, a leader of this land. Great wisdom will fall on your people. The people that once tried to destroy you will look to you to lead them away from their own destruction.

8

The Favor of Esther

After writing Book One, I got invited to speak at the women's prison. I really liked those girls there; they are good people. God showed me something about these women that paralleled Queen Esther that probably is the same for a lot of us. So if you can relate, this chapter is for you.

Sometimes we feel like we are in a prison being punished because we did something bad, but what if you are there because God thinks you are beautiful, and He captured you because He really wants your attention.

If you can, read Esther 2:1–18. I would type it, but it's too long so I will have to paraphrase and then explain: The king gets mad at his queen and dumps her. Now he's looking for a new queen. He sends his soldiers out, and they capture the young beautiful women in his territory and take them into his palace, no longer to return home to their former life.

They are treated with the best of foods, oils, and perfumes for a year; the first six months with oil of myrrh, then following six months with perfumes and preparations for beautifying women. At the end of the year, they are presented to the king, and the one who pleases him the most becomes his queen.

Esther was a young orphan girl being raised by her uncle. She was very pretty. She got captured by the soldiers and brought to the palace. She found favor with the king's eunuch who was custodian over them, and he treated her with more favor than the others. He wanted her to win. She was beautiful both inside and out, and when she went before the king, she pleased him, and he made her his queen.

It may sound silly, but have you ever felt arrested by God? It's like He has His thumb on you, and no matter what you do, you can't get out from under it. I heard a sermon about this once, and I thought it sure sounded like me. I've tried to leave this place so many times, but I'm still here.

Even when things were good and I was making good money building houses, I was buying tools and setting myself up for a future move. Then the bottom fell out of the housing market and now half of my place is full of power tools, a real man cave. It's hard, but at the same time, there is favor.

I was sitting here last night thinking about how much I have changed since I've been here; God has changed me so much. I got so humbled before Him and thought about just how beautiful and worthy He is. I'm fifty years old, and I feel like I'm just barely starting to grow up.

Women know a lot more about oils and perfumes and beautifying things than I do, so I can only say things the way I see it. In the beginning, I was so messed up, I was hard like leather. I remember Pastor David taking me to church meetings, and they were just too much for me. But somehow, God has oiled me and softened me up.

I look at things now and wonder why they used to bother me so much. Now I go to churches like I use to go to the bars. I have my home group, then I go church hopping, and I enjoy it more. I love God's holy wine, and I do admire God's people. I have had my share of hard times, and sometimes I wonder why God keeps putting up with me, but apparently He just dumps more oil on me, and we go the rounds again.

Then there are changes in my character that in a sense make me smell better. I can give one quick example. There were times in my past that when I got a small job, and I didn't have money, I would get a deposit and keep the deposit money to buy beer. I'd write a hot check to cover materials, then hurry to get the job done, and beat the check to the bank.

It worked most of the time, but it doesn't allow you to take extra time to do a good job and not cut corners. I just got a little job the other day for a lady on limited income. It was so small that I couldn't ask for a deposit, but I didn't have enough money. It was so tempting to write a check; I did write one out, but I didn't use it.

I decided to buy what I had money for and hoped it would all work out. It turned out that the guy before me didn't do a good job, and I had to fix his stuff before I could do my job. It took all day, and I had just enough material for what I needed. So that gave me the night to figure out how to come up with the rest of the money for what I needed.

Well, I couldn't come up with it, and I didn't know what to do. I didn't want to borrow any, and it didn't make sense to hock anything. So I prayed and trusted God, believing that this was a test on seeing if I would do the right thing, even in a small matter.

I was stressed when morning came, and I was asking God what to do. I saw something on my table that I was going to return and get my money back from several months ago and didn't. Then it dawned on me of other things I had, and together it all gave me enough to get what I needed. So now I wasn't in a rush, and I wasn't racing a check to the bank.

I got the job done and even did extra things for her. She thanked me and told me about how bad of an attitude she's had because of carpenters who ripped her off. She told me that what I did for her showed my character and restored her faith in that there were honest people still out there. That made me feel good, and I think God thought the same thing of me too.

Favor is a hard thing to explain. It's like everything I used to touch went wrong. I always had the feeling of impending doom. I remember when I would leave for even a weekend, I would be afraid of coming home because of wondering what went wrong while I was gone. I've been gone for months lately, came home, and still all has been well.

Coincidences happen that are beyond the natural, almost every day, which show me God is there. Mistakes I've made turned out to be for the better. Things that looked bad turned out good. Favor is really important to see and recognize. God talks in many ways. Favor is one of His voices. Not very long ago, He told me that hard times were coming, and we need to learn to see His favor now so that we could recognize Him when it comes because it's in His favor that we are going to make it through.

If you read all of Esther, there came a time that she had to come before the king, and if the king didn't find favor for her, it meant her death. He found favor for her and gave her victory over her enemies. That's the favor we have with God. Even when we feel so unworthy, He listens and doesn't turn us away and fights for us.

Something I have noticed when we first come to God and get saved is we have a lot of favor, even though the devil still tests us. It's like God declares favor over us as He deals with that black cloud of judgments coming against us from all the bad things we used to do.

The Bible says that we will reap what we have sown, and that once we're a Christian, we are held more accountable. If you are like how I used to be and keep going back to the old world, these judgments don't get removed easily until you've been really tested and proven that you have changed.

But once the judgments are dealt with, life goes so much easier. God still has grace beyond grace and rules in our favor, but backsliding is a tough road to go.

I have a friend, and we've been partying buddies and have worked together for over thirty years. He's put up with me being sober and still worked with me. He got a DUI and chose to do drug court for two years. I thought that was a blessing because I was watching him slowly die and couldn't do anything about it. He did good staying sober for those two years. I knew he planned to go back to drinking once it was over, but I hoped he wouldn't. During that time, he had such bad luck, it seemed like every time he turned around, something went wrong, and he was looking at going to jail.

My church group liked him and prayed for him every time, and God would favor him, and things always worked out. That's where I saw that cloud over him that I was talking about, and how much favor God had, and He delivered him every time. A big test came, and he quit and took off. He went back to the old ways and had a rough road to hoe. I didn't give up; I think God was still after him and maybe even steering him. I'm going to write about him in Book Three. He died, but a story is there, and I believe God saved him.

I've been watching my friends die one by one after being told that if they go back to the old life they will die. They go back, and they die. It would be baffling to me except I've been there too, so I know what it's like. But how do I tell them that there is a better way before it's too late. Maybe that's what these books are for.

9

It's A New Day

In this chapter, I'm going to be bold. I believe God has been showing me something over the years that I have never had the courage to tell anybody. I did a test run on a couple of people now to see if they could shoot me down, but so far I'm okay.

I've been a carpenter for over thirty years now and most of it has been self-taught. I've worked for good people, learned a lot, and through the years, I'd pick up things from other people that would improve my skills. But most of the time, I just figured it out, and through trial and error, got good at it.

Sometimes I got in over my head, but one thing I've always done was prayed and asked for God's help at the beginning of every job and every day, and He has been faithful to help me.

I'm not trying to brag now but to make a point; the second house that I built was a big house in the rich area of town. When I finished and got it inspected, the inspector said that it was the first big house that he had inspected, which he hadn't found one single problem, and he passed it. My confidence went up after that.

It's been the same in my Christian life. I never went to Bible college. I had several pastors whom I've learned a lot from, and I learn a lot from people, but mostly I figure it out. My way of studying is different than most.

I can't break open the Bible and just study subjects very well. My brain gets going on so many rabbit trails that before long I'm in a mental exhaustion and have to shut it down. You can probably see that in the way I write. My method of learning now is just reading and listening for the Holy Spirit to teach me things.

When I hear new things from people, I usually put it on a mental shelf, and if I can read through the whole Bible without it having any discrepancies, then I'll adopt it. I read through the Bible at least once a year, and I've done that for almost all of my Christian life.

Like I've said before, I also watch a movie called *The Gospel of John* that I don't get tired of. I've watched it an average of at least once a week over the last six years, so conservatively I could say I've watched it at least 250 times. There's a way of learning that comes when the Gospel is repeated over and over again, and I still keep seeing new things. That is a benefit of being in my cave. It's also a result from my experience that I had with God six years ago that I wrote in Book One. I can't get enough of Jesus.

I believe my calling is like that servant prophet whom Elisha sent to Jehu to anoint to be king over Israel. It's like I get these packages to take to people, like preachers, and they have the keys to open it and can preach whole sermons out of it. Sometimes I don't even know; I just say something that I think God is telling me, and it unlocks a whole series of revelation in someone else.

One day I was at a church, and during worship service, we were getting ready to sing a song by Petra about going into the holy of holies. The pastor told us to let ourselves go and enter into the presence of God, so I did. It was easy because I love that song. As we were singing, God took me in a vision. He lifted me clear up in the atmosphere, like past the satellites, into His heaven. From there, I saw a bright heavenly sun dawning. I was singing in the spirit, and it was like I was singing in harmony with all the angels of heaven, heralding in the dawn of a new day. The sun wasn't just coming up, it was fully up.

I couldn't find a place or get the courage to say anything, so I just pondered on what it meant. When I got home, I picked up where I left off reading in a book by George Warnock called *From Tent to Temple*. He was talking about the tabernacle and temples that had been built by the Jews all have the main entrance facing east. That it spoke of a promise of a new day: "Unto you that fear My name shall the Sun of righteousness arise with healing in His wings" (Mal. 4:2).

Then I got excited, we were singing a song about going into the holy of holies (God's temple) and then being lifted up to see the heavenly morning sun, and then reading this, I figured God was telling me something.

I believe we are now in a new day. Not at the threshold of it, but "in it." Life on earth will never be the same as it was. So what does it mean to be in a new day? Well, it might challenge you, but I think I have an answer.

I believe we are in the return of Jesus. I believe when Jesus came the first time, it was a pattern of how He is going to come this second time, which culminates in, instead of, His final return to heaven; it will be His final physical return from heaven. I don't have it all worked out. One day maybe I can write it all, but I think I can give you enough that, if you agree, you will be able to unpack this yourself because it is so simple, and the parallels will start unfolding.

Luke 2:41–52 is about when Jesus was twelve years old, and His parents weren't keeping track of Him and left Him in Jerusalem; He was lingering behind. When they realized He was missing, they went back and found Him in the temple. He was astounding the teachers there with His knowledge, and He was ready to be about His Father's business. He was ready to start His ministry, but His mother said no. I believe, through the inspiration of God the Father and her wisdom, she knew it was not His time. He would have been crucified before He had seen His sixteenth birthday. So He submitted to her.

Then He went through His teenage years and twenties. The Bible doesn't say much about this time except that He grew in wisdom and stature and in favor with God and man. I call these "God's vacation years." It was a time that God got to spend with man, walking as a man, and not having the scrutiny of historians polluting His every move with their false judgments. This was His time to be with man, like He used to be in the garden.

Then John the Baptist came, in the spirit of Elijah, to restore all things. He taught repentance from sin, turning to God, and that the Messiah was coming. He also brought to light peoples' sins like he did King Herod, about it being wrong for him to have his brother's wife. Then when Jesus came, John chose to decrease so that Jesus could increase.

Now to draw a parallel. When Jesus was twelve, that time represented the early church; it was young and ready to go and minister. Their knowledge was astounding, and they are why we have the New Testament today. I think what we lack today that they had was the council of the Apostles. Some churches have their denominational apostles, but we need the real apostles of the real church to have a council to reestablish the right doctrines again that we all should live by.

I'm not a history buff, but after them, we went into the Dark Ages for hundreds of years. From what I know, we don't know a lot about the church during that period, the same like we don't know much about Jesus's life while He was growing up. Then John the Baptist came to restore things and make the crooked places straight. These are kind of like the movements we have been having in the last two hundred years or so, which brought back faith and healing to the church. Jesus getting baptized by John, and the Holy Spirit descending upon Him, represents the bringing back of the baptism of the Holy Spirit.

The corruption in the church that's been brought out now is like John bringing out the people's sins, especially Herod's, and preaching repentance to them. But the time for us is coming when Jesus is going to cleanse the church like He did the temple, and it won't be just a onetime event. Jesus cleansed the temple at the beginning of His ministry and at the end; I think He went after them every time He went into the temple.

When Jesus began His ministry, John the Baptist said that he must decrease so that Jesus would increase. I wonder when this great move of God happens, how many church leaders will say that. People will be gathering in homes, fields, stadiums, etc. and not necessarily in denominations. As the denominations begin to lose money and power, what will they do?

Will they become like the Pharisees and try to put a stop to it, to put Jesus to death? I see this could unite the world's religious leaders to a common purpose, causing enemies to become friends because it will happen in every religious system of the world. The tree of life, and the tree of death, will be coming into full bloom together.

I believe we are now paralleling the time when Jesus was gathering His disciples, just before the marriage feast where He turned the water into wine. I believe what Jesus is doing now, in the spirit, is gathering His disciples to evangelize the world.

A parallel too is Joshua. In Joshua 5:13–14 (NKJV), it says,

> And it came to pass, when Joshua was by Jericho, that he lifted his eyes and looked, and behold, a Man stood opposite him with His sword drawn in His hand. And Joshua went to Him and said to Him, "Are you for us or for our adversaries?" So He said, "No, but as Commander of the army of the Lord I have now come." And Joshua fell on his face to the earth and worshipped, and said to Him, "What does my Lord say to His servant?"

The time of going around the mountain is over. Jesus is going into the promised land. The man who led Joshua is the same as Jesus leading His disciples today. The disciples will be like Joshua, fathers and mothers, to this new generation that is going in to inhabit the full kingdom of God. This new generation isn't just young people but young believers; it doesn't matter how old you are. They will go from babies to warriors overnight.

Another parallel is the men and women now who are like King David, who hid away, waiting for the reign of

King Saul to be over. I believe Jesus is calling men and women from all around the world to get ready to leave everything and follow Him. The Bible does say that we are seated with Him in heavenly places. Now it's our job in history to be the ones interceding, like the bowls of prayers being poured out before the throne!

Jesus has been raising up intercessory prayer groups and 24-7 houses of worship, like Kansas City's IHOPU, everywhere around the world. What if we are at it, and now more than ever, our words carry weight before God's throne. If this is true, and if we are cursing (word curses) instead of blessing and interceding, then we are in trouble. But I know there are people whom Jesus is formed in, who can stand before the throne and intercede, and you might be one.

Like I said, I believe we are at the time of being at the marriage feast, where they were out of wine, and Jesus's mother, Mary, told the servants to do whatever Jesus told them to do. Jesus told her that His time has not yet come. I think He was enjoying being a man and hanging out with His friends; He was not ready to go get killed yet. But His mother saw all the signs, and I believe the Father was telling her it was time, so she released Him from her authority and gave Him back to the Father, sending Him into His ministry.

I believe where we are is waiting for "mother" to release Jesus into His ministry. His people have been tested, and they've overcome. They're tired of the denominational walls, and they are ready to become one.

The next thing that we will see is the water of the Word getting turned into the wine of the Word. Then the world will pay attention and start gathering to where Jesus is, in His people. I think everything that is written in the Gospels is a prophecy of what will happen when Jesus begins His move, except it will end with His triumphant return. It's like a prophecy within a true life story.

It's seems like we've worked and worked to the point that we are tired, and we just can't hardly get anybody saved anymore. In my group, we haven't had any new believers in over ten years. It almost seems like I've forgotten the basics because there is no one around to teach them. I say this because I hear it in other places too.

But I think it is like the disciples who were out fishing when Jesus first called them to follow Him, and they caught nothing, but then Jesus showed up. He told them to throw their nets out again, and they caught more than what their nets could hold, and the nets began to tear. I think that represents the first wave of the revival that's coming. The church isn't ready for it, and we don't know how to hold together, but we will figure it out.

At the end of Jesus's ministry, before He ascended, Peter went back to fishing, and that night they caught nothing. Jesus showed up and told them to throw their nets out again. They caught a great amount of fish, and this time their nets didn't tear. The church will get it together. It will be supernatural, but we will do it. We liken churches coming together like knots being tied together in a net.

The dropout rate of pastors right now is astounding. Most of it is burnout from a dying religious system. I wonder how much guilt they feel. God is going to restore them. It's like Peter who, after denying knowing Jesus three times—really two sets of three—felt so guilty that he went back to his trade, fishing, instead of telling people about Jesus's resurrection.

When Jesus came to Peter and asked him if he loved Him those three times, it brought up Peter's failure, but then Jesus restored Peter by telling him in John 21:18–19 (NKJV), saying,

> Most assuredly, I say to you, when you were younger, you girded yourself and walked where you wished; but when you are *old*, you will stretch out your hands, and another will gird you and carry you where you do not wish. This He spoke, signifying by what death he would glorify God. And when He had spoken this, He said to him, "Follow Me." (emphasis added)

I can see Peter raising his hands in victory, saying, "Yes, once He told me that I would fail Him, and I did. Now He tells me that I will be strong and stand for Him, so I know I will." Kind of a cheerful way of getting told that you are going to get killed one day.

Something I see really cool about Peter after this is in Acts 12. Herod had just killed James, John's brother, and he went after Peter and threw him in prison to kill him after the Passover. The night before Herod was going to bring him out and kill him, Peter was sound asleep, and an angel had to strike him in order to wake him up so that he could set him free.

If I knew I was going to be killed the next morning, I don't think I would be sleeping very much, if at all. I believe Peter remembered Jesus's words when He told him, "When you are *old*, you will stretch out your hands." Well, Peter wasn't old; he was somewhere in his early twenties, so he knew he wasn't going to die. He *believed* Jesus. Plus, he had gotten the baptism in the Holy Spirit, which is what changed him and made him strong. He stood for Jesus and didn't run; God restored him, which must have made him feel really good.

People who have lost their hope in church will be restored. I see this move in the story of the Samaritan woman at the well in John 4:4–42. When Jesus talked to her, her response was, "When the Messiah comes, He will tell us everything." It was like the truth was so messed up in her day, just like it seems in ours, that she lived by what was right in her own eyes, even though she had a heart for God.

Notice Jesus didn't condemn her for having five husbands and living in adultery with the man she had now. Then she went and told the people in her town about Him, and the whole town came to see Him. He spent time with them, and they believed in Him.

I could go on and on. The blind will see, lepers cleansed, doubters will come face-to-face with the truth. They are all representatives of moves of the Spirit that are going to happen in the final return of Jesus, which I believe we are in now.

10

Cannonballs

Since I've stepped out of the boat in Book One and a few steps out on the water now, I might as well go all the way with what I got. What if God is showing me things that I'm supposed to tell and I don't, I'd probably be doing you a disservice. This dream here is what kept me writing.

I dreamed that I was trying to sign my name on a receipt for a book. The book was in my left hand, and I had a pen in my right. The paper I was signing kept moving around, and my name wasn't coming out very good. I started to get mad, and I threw the book down to grab hold of the paper so that I could write better.

When I threw the book down, it bounced off the table and almost hit a lady standing across from me. Her husband was there, and he started rebuking me about my temper and because I almost hit his wife with the book. Then I woke up. While waking up, I was saying over and over, "Faith without works is dead."

It took me a while, but then I figured out that God was telling me that if I'm worried about how my name looks, I will never get this book written. And if I lay this book down, I could end up hurting other people. If I don't start writing, then my faith is dead. So I started writing. I still had no idea what; I get inspired and then I write, then I go blank, then I start praying, and it comes. I named this book the whirlwind because I'm all over the place, I don't know who I'm writing to, and I have no story line. But it seems to be coming together by itself.

This chapter is going to be about principalities falling down and intercessory prayer. I want to start out with a vision I had, after a Burn, about Curtis when he prays. Similar to what I said in the last chapter, let Curtis represent the intercessors of the church.

In the vision, I'm sitting up in God's throne with Him at about His chest level. I'm not very big. I'm looking down over His knees, and the floor of His throne room is made out of clouds, the third heaven. As I'm sitting there, I keep seeing these little black cannonballs popping up out of the clouds, going up about Him knee-high, and then falling back into the clouds. They just keep popping up all over the place before His throne, then falling back down.

I'm wondering what these cannonballs mean, so I asked God. In a moment, I'm back down on earth standing beside Curtis just after he had finished praying. I looked up, and I could see the second heaven, Satan's realm, and it has these holes blown through it from Curtis's prayers. The holes were big, like they were shot through with giant cannonballs, but in God's throne room, He's so big that they looked small.

Next, I'm back up in His throne where I was, and another cannonball popped up, and then God freeze-frames it. I can see writings on the ball, which are Curtis's prayers, then God unfreezes it, and it falls back into the clouds. God showed me that He sees your prayers, and that He does take notice of them.

But then something changes because now the cannonballs pop up out of the clouds and they land in Jesus's right hand. His hand is turned up, cupped, and laying on the right armrest of His throne. God says a new level of authority has been put on you, which has elevated your authority in prayer.

Now Jesus is filling His hand with these cannonballs that you are firing up, and when He is ready, He is going to hurl these cannonballs down with great fury and with pinpoint accuracy. Suddenly, Satan is going to know the wrath of God with devastating destruction from your intercessory prayers.

Your cannonballs did damage to the devil going up and then they will again, as God hurls them back down on him. Then I ask God about the earlier cannonballs, what happened to them when they fell back into the clouds? He told me not to worry, that He will not let even one of your words fall to the ground.

Now let me tell you a Bible story in my version. This is all thinking in my own head, but if I am right, it could give you direction on how to pray. If nothing else, it might challenge you to think on your own. I will build a foundation first.

> How you are fallen from heaven, O Lucifer, son of the morning! How you are cut down to the ground, you who weakened the nations! For you have said in your heart: "I will ascend into heaven, I will exalt my throne above the stars of God, I will also sit on the mount of the congregation on the farthest sides of the north, I will ascend above the heights of the clouds, I will be like the Most High." Yet you shall be brought down to Sheol, to the lowest depths of the pit." (Isaiah 14:12–15, NKJV)

> And *Jesus* said unto them, "I saw Satan fall like lightning from heaven." (Luke 10:18, NKJV)

> And Jesus cried out again with a loud voice, and yielded up His spirit. Then, behold, the veil of the temple was torn in two from top to bottom; and the earth quaked, and the rocks were split. (Matthew 27:50–51, NKJV)

> For we do not wrestle against flesh and blood, but against principalities, against powers, against the rulers of the darkness of this age, against spiritual hosts of wickedness in the heavenly places. (Ephesians 6:12, NKJV)

In Jesus's day, where would Satan's throne have been on the earth? Since Satan was so set on having his throne above God's throne, wouldn't it make sense that it would be above

The Holiness of God

the temple, directly above the holy of holies. Herod's throne was powerless really, Pontius Pilot had more authority than him. Yet neither one of them would dare go into the holy of holies.

Pyramiding down from Satan's throne would be the principalities, powers, dark rulers, and hosts of wickedness.

Now let's go to the day of Jesus's crucifixion, like where I started this book. Satan is there with all his demons, and you could imagine the torment he's putting Jesus through, and there is no mercy. Jesus is now the devil's trophy, stuck up on a hill by Jerusalem, for the whole world to see. The Son of God is reduced to being worth no more than a worm by those He created and loved.

Satan is standing in his throne at the top of his kingdom, with his hands raised in victory, and is absorbing the worship of all his hosts. Then Jesus dies. Unknowing to Satan that he had just defeated himself, the authority he held disappeared, and immediately his throne fell. He fell like lightning and crashed through the veil separating the holies of holies, splitting it in two from top to bottom. He hit the ground so hard that the earth shook and rocks split.

There's another really good teaching that I heard about the time when Jesus told His disciples that He saw Satan fall like lightning. It was when the disciples returned after He sent them out two by two, telling them to heal the sick, cleanse the lepers, raise the dead, cast out demons, etc. They came back saying that even the demons obeyed them.

I hope I can say this right, but when the disciple obeyed the word to go, they went in the anointing that broke the bondages of Satan that the people were in, and it brought down his kingdom and brought in God's kingdom. I think Satan's kingdom has bitten the dust many times, and it's time to do it again.

So what if the church is rising up? What if we now walk in a new level of authority? What if we are learning how to blow holes through the principalities of heaven, and they are breaking up and coming down? What if the people held by these principalities then are no longer under their sway? What if that's how revival begins?

Well, I believe it is already happening. What I am about to say I can't prove, but this is what I believe God has told me. Earlier this year there was an earthquake off Japan's coast that created a tsunami, which destroyed everything in its path as it hit Japan's shores. God told me that this wasn't His judgment against Japan. That it was because of the church's intercession, that demonic powers fell and had spread across the land in a rage, destroying everything in their path. But following it will come a revival that they have never seen, and now that revival has been happening.

I'm not saying every earthquake is principalities falling, but somehow the spiritual and the physical realms are connected. And when the demonic forces get mad, they can stir things up just as well as God can.

The Holiness of God

God told me that judgments are coming to America though that will be in direct proportion to how we didn't help Japan. He said that He was going to go right through the middle of America. Well, 2011 has had some of the worst snows, floods, droughts, fires, and tornadoes on record going right through the middle of us.

God does love America. He made that real plain to me one time. I will write about that in the next book because it's another story. But the Bible says He chastises those He loves, and if there is no chastisement then we're really in trouble.

He said that principalities are then going to be coming down because the real church is repenting, and that we need to pray and intercede. That when these principalities fall, they are going to go across our land in a rage, and that we need to raise up a *wall* against them to restrain them.

I didn't understand this word, and I got my courage up and told my church group. Then that night in my Bible reading, the spot where I was reading at was in Ezekiel 22:30 (NKJV) that said, "So I sought for a man among them who would make a *wall*, and stand in the gap before Me on behalf of the land, that I should not destroy it; but I found none" (emphasis added). There are two things happening: God's judgments on sin, and principalities falling because the church is rising up.

Through the years, I've learned lessons about the differences between warring against principalities and interceding. I've watched churches bind principalities and now they no longer exist, but the principalities are still standing. Even after fifteen years, some of the people are still hurt and want nothing to do with church. We just didn't know what we were getting into, and we got knocked on our butts.

Spiritual warfare is not a game, and you better be prepared to pay a price and walk a life of constant repentance with no openings in your armor between you and your whole church. I've heard people talk tough, and it sounded good on paper. But we are not ready for that kind of warfare, at least not yet, but it will come.

There is a way that is just as powerful, if not more, that we can weaken the enemy until we can knock it down, and that is in intercessory prayer. See, God has a soft spot, and if we can get to that soft spot and get God to rule in our favor, anything is possible.

I heard a preaching once that answered a question that I had, and it opened up a whole new side of God that I had never seen before. It's in Exodus 19. I won't write it out, but I will explain the part I'm talking about.

I think everybody knows the story of Moses and the Ten Commandments. Moses had brought the children of Israel out of Egypt to Mount Sinai to meet with God. God told them that when He comes onto the mountain to meet with them, they were not to go near the mountain at all or they would die. Only Moses could go up. Verses 21–24 confused me because after Moses went up to God, God was more

The Holiness of God

lenient and said if Israel came up to see Him, *many*, instead of *all*, would die. Also to let the priest come too.

Moses reminded God that He had said that no one was to come up. God got mad and basically told him to get away from Him and let no one else come up after that. It became that way from then on too, including only the high priest could go into the holy of holies once a year, and he had better be pure. So why did God get mad?

Then I learned that God wasn't mad; He was hurt. After all that He had done for them, they still did not know Him. They weren't willing to ask, or risk their lives, to see Him. It's like God was saying no but really meaning yes and just wanting to see how much we really wanted Him. That's God's soft spot. He wants to be loved! Out of over a million people, not one person risked it.

King David saw this when he brought the ark to his city to be with him. The ark represents God's presence. But it was against God's law; He had a temple made for Himself somewhere else. God did get mad in the way the ark was brought, but not to where it was brought. Animal's blood had to be shed every six steps the ark was carried; the number six represents man. There is only one prescribed way to carry the ark, and that represents Jesus, by His blood, being the only way to God. It's not negotiable.

But King David loved God; he wanted Him near him so that he could be with Him whenever he wanted. David set up a 24-77 praise and worship to God, and it touched His soft spot. God honored him and allowed Himself to stay, and His new place was now only in a tent with everybody. God prefers hearts more than buildings.

Then, from that place, David conquered all of his enemies and ushered in the greatest kingdom that had ever existed. But David had a weakness—women—and the devil got him. It eventually brought down his whole kingdom. Jesus brought us a new way: intercession. Even though it's not new, it contained a secret—through intercession we can reverse the curse. We can turn the curse of death back to life.

I'm not an expert at this yet, but I can tell you what I have discovered. There's a place when you get into worship that you fall so in love with God that it melts Him. And even if He is so mad that He could spit, you can stop Him in His tracks, and instead of getting punished, He favors you and fights for you.

I believe we are in a new day, and it's time to change. I think the more we come together as a people and worship God and intercede, the more we will see things change, and even change God's judgments. My example for this is Paul in Acts 27: he was a prisoner being taken to Rome on a ship. It was late in the year and not good for sailing. God showed him that if they sailed, it would end in the loss of their ship and their lives. Paul told them this, but they took him and sailed anyway.

Then a big storm came up, and it blew them out to sea for days. They had given up hope and threw everything overboard. But Paul interceded for them, and God changed His mind and gave Paul all their lives. Even though they lost the ship, they all made it to shore and lived. Paul got to spend some time with them after that, and I'm sure they heard the gospel, but it doesn't say if any of them got saved.

I had a prophet tell me not long ago that I accomplish more when I say less. He had never met me and knew nothing about me. He said that I had a gift, that God would draw me away in music, and that I could lock myself away for hours on end and pray and intercede.

I didn't know I was doing that. I knew I could spend hours and hours in music, abandoning myself in God and loving it. Every once in a while, someone would come up in my mind, and I would pray for them, but I didn't consider myself a praying person. Then I realized that the very fact that I was abandoning myself to God wholeheartedly in worship is in itself prayer and intercession.

God knew my heart, and He knows how much I care even when I don't know how to express it, but I do make an effort. Not as good as I hear other people who can pray, but my spirit prays, and God hears. That's what happens when you capture God's heart. I know that if we can start gathering and worshiping together, becoming one and interceding, we will be removing what gives principalities the right to stand, and they will fall.

11

11/11

It was two years ago today that I started Book One. Today is also my birthday; I'm fifty-one today, so for me 11/11 has always been a good day. I wanted to talk about a dream that I had, but I have no idea what the dream was.

I had a dream, and in my dream I was realizing that it was a God dream, and that I needed to remember it. It was really important. As I was waking up, I was saying in my mind 11/11 over and over so that I could remember it because there was something about those numbers that would remind me of what the dream was about. As I woke up and opened my eyes, I looked at my clock at the far end of my room, and the time was 11:11. So I figured God was telling me something, and I got up to write it down.

But no matter how I tried, I couldn't remember it. The only thing I had was that something really big was going to happen, and that when it did happen, there would no longer be any more need for writing books. Everybody would know.

I was sitting at my computer desk, and since I couldn't remember, I decided to check my e-mail. Sometimes my memory works when I'm thinking about something else. In my mail, I had been forwarded an e-mail that talked about the significance of the date 11/11 in history. Well that just blew my mind. Three things just happened that had to do with 11/11 within about five minutes, so I e-mailed everybody on my list telling them about it and forwarded that e-mail.

I don't have much of anything else to say about that; it's just another one of those things that stand out in my life that tells me something really big is coming. All my life, I've had a sense that someday something big was going to happen, and that when it did happen, life as we know it would never be the same again. It was like we were going to wake up one morning and everything was going to be changed, never to be the same again.

So, ever since I was a teenager, my goal was to become self-sufficient. I wanted to build my own house and have land, have my own well and power, have farm animals and horses, etc. I guess that's why I've learned to do everything myself. But my life was always dominated by drugs and alcohol, and I never achieved that.

So maybe I am achieving it in the spirit, and if I could leave you remembering three important things, it would be this: read your Bible, hear God for yourself, and think for yourself. There is still a deception coming that the Bible says is so powerful that even God's elect would be deceived if it were possible.

Paul wrote in Acts 20:28–31 (NKJV),

> Therefore take heed to yourselves and to all the flock, among which the Holy Spirit has made you overseers, to shepherd the church of God which He purchased with His own blood. For I know this, that after my departure savage wolves will come in among you, not sparing the flock. Also from among yourselves men will rise up, speaking perverse things, to draw away disciples after themselves. Therefore watch, and remember that for three years I did not cease to warn everyone night and day with tears.

I had a dream last night, and that is why I'm saying this. I dreamed that I was at a lady's house, and she had a piano. She was good at playing old gospel music. A new kind of music came out, and in order for her to play it, she needed to offset her string table just enough out of alignment but still be able to have her keys hit right. So we tweaked it, and then I moved on.

This is weird. But next, I was at a guy's house, and he wanted work done on his toilet. There was a new kind of toilet paper that had come out, and it only worked if you offset your toilet over its hole, so I moved it and went on to my next job.

Next there was a white rug that had gotten stained, and the stain was growing in the rug, slowly turning the whole thing black. I had to wash the rug before the stain dried or the stain would become permanent.

Then there was something that was broke, and it had to be returned to the store to get fixed. It was for a pastor, and I told him that we needed to go to that store today while they were still opened. He said that we still had plenty of time, and we could do it tomorrow. Tomorrow came, and when we went to the store, it was closed down permanently, and we were no longer able to get that thing fixed.

Then I went back past the lady with the piano, and she was angry. She had been playing her new music and was fine, then she wanted to go back and play her old gospel songs, but they wouldn't play because her piano was tweaked.

Then I was at the guy's house with the toilet, and there was a line of people going to his bathroom, and he was angry. He went back to the old toilet paper, and it kept plugging up his toilet, so he was constantly running to it with a plunger to fix it. Then I realized that there was something wrong with all this new stuff that was coming out. So I started doing some investigative reporting. I discovered that there was some kind of underground group that was bringing in stuff by stealth to realign things, and that they were an enemy.

I took what I found to a newspaper group, and one guy wanted to join me, but the other held up his hand, showing the ring on his finger, and with fear in his eyes said that if he did this, they would not only hurt him but his family too. It was like he already knew that they were there, and that they were extremely bad people. Then I woke up.

The Holiness of God

When I woke up, I had this overwhelming feeling that something is coming that is powerful, and it will try to tweak and realign our faith. If we encounter it, we will have only a short window of time to reject it because once it got in, it was so powerful that we wouldn't be able to get it out. And that the structure that is doing this is already in place; they are doing this by stealth, and that we are in a war.

It was a strange dream. I was going to forget about it, but I've been learning that dreams that make no sense, after a while, start making sense. So sometimes, I write down just enough to remember them. Usually, they are so real, and I remember them so well that I don't have to write them down at all. That's mostly how I know if it's a God dream.

The number 11 represents transition, and it seems to be my number. I believe that we are in a time of transitioning from old wineskins into new wineskins. But we have to beware of the counterfeit. I have learned that a lot of times before God does something, a counterfeit will come along to get us offtrack. It's hard because sometimes it sways us to wait too long, or sometimes it sways us to move too soon. But expect a counterfeit to come.

I believe we are stepping out of an old age of grace into a new age of grace. Time and eternity have kissed. A dividing line is coming. The tree of life and the tree of death are coming into full bloom side by side. There will no longer be a middle-of-the-road or riding the fence.

I heard a preaching not long ago that I thought was really good, and it fit with what I was seeing, so I adopted it. He talked about the angel in Revelation 14:6–7 (NKJV)

> Then I saw another angel flying in the midst of heaven, having the everlasting gospel to preach to those who dwell on the earth- to every nation, tribe, tongue, and people- saying with a loud voice, "Fear God and give glory to Him, for the hour of His judgment has come; and worship Him who made heaven and earth, the sea and springs of water."

I've always wondered about that angel, and the way he explained it made so much sense to me. He said that when that angel is released, he will not be preaching to the world in an audible voice, but he will be speaking spiritually to every person on the earth, into the very core of their being.

Then the person will choose to either accept Jesus or reject Him from within their spirit or subconscious being. If a person accepts the angel's message, then someone will come along and preach to them the Gospel message. They will have a stirring inside them that comes from deep within, and a knowing that this is right, like they've heard this before. They will already be predisposed to receiving the Gospel. This is what will bring in the last great harvest. I thought that this was so cool, and for me, it fits

But that's the final call. If the angel comes over a person, and he rejects his message, that dividing line will come across him and the grace for him is over. This is where grace

The Holiness of God

changes. The person who receives the Gospel will go from being the worst sinner to walking in spotless righteousness seemingly overnight.

To the person who rejects the Gospel, even the good that they do will fade away, and then they will become altogether corrupt. It's like the wealth of the wicked will be taken away from them and given to the poor.

Now is the time, more than ever, that we need to be interceding for everyone, asking God that He would see everybody that we are praying for, which should be the world, to get the obstacles moved out of the way from them so that they will have the freedom to be drawn to and choose life.

We need to find our secret place with God and get into His presence, His soft spot; from there, we can fight for people. This is the time that I think, when we are in the next life, we will look back and wish we had prayed more.

Lean into the Holy Spirit and listen and learn to think for yourself. I used to think that because we had these great Bible colleges, and they had all the years of knowledge and wisdom in the deepest things of God, that they had it all figured out, and that we were just too small to know God. But that's not true.

I think God has hidden knowledge in plain sight, saved especially for these last days, that is so simple that, if we complicate it, we will miss it. Like the story of creation in the first chapters of Genesis, it's like a riddle. It solves itself by itself, within the boundaries of itself, and is the foundation that supports the rest of the Bible.

From the very beginning, God makes us think and teaches us how He thinks. The idea that we can let our pastor do all of our thinking is not going to be good, especially if for some reason they get removed, and we find ourselves on our own.

This paragraph is for someone. There's a quote I heard once that says "There is no such thing as illegitimate children, only illegitimate parents." God has known you before the foundation of the world, and there is a book in heaven written with your name on it, so "come and fulfill your destiny."

Well, I have a lot of things percolating for the next book. It's been a process of two steps forward and one step backward. Writing is a lot harder than what a person would think. But I can get totally absorbed in it, and hopefully I'm doing a good job. I've already found out that it's hard to please everybody, so I'm trying to keep it simple. Anyway, thanks for reading this, and hopefully I will see you in the next book.